A Captivating Read! Keeler, a consummate listener and storyteller, has collected vivid memories of ordinary people caught up in World War II in Europe, various islands of the vast Pacific, and even back home in America. Drawing upon his life experiences and in-depth interviews, his retelling of amazing, harrowing, humorous, and inspiring personal accounts of WW II, capture what it is to be human when inhumanity overwhelms the whole world."

—**David Martyn, Author**

"*This book is an amazing collection of compelling stories from real people who were involved directly or indirectly in WWII. I appreciate these stories because my father was in Europe and the Philippines in the mid-1940s. He didn't talk much about the war so these stories give me a glimpse into his war experience, which I know affected his later life. Some stories are humorous, some are poignant, some are unimaginable...I laughed and I cried. The author has extensive personal knowledge of the Pacific Islands and associated war history plus a talent for drawing people out with an eye for a good story. I found all of the stories fascinating, and I have enthusiastically recommended this book to several of my friends.*"

—**Judy, Bellingham, WA**

HEROES, HORROR, & HUMOR IN WORLD WAR II

A COLLECTION OF PERSONAL TALES

Geoffrey S. Keeler

HEROES, HORROR, & HUMOR IN WORLD WAR II
A Collection of Personal Tales

First edition, published 2022

By Geoffrey S. Keeler
Cover Image provided by Calbom Family
Cover Design Reprospace, LLC
Copyright © 2022, Geoffrey S. Keeler

Paperback ISBN-978-1-952685-37-8

All rights reserved. No part of this book may be reproduced or transmitted in any form or by any means, electronic or mechanical, including photocopying, recording or by any information storage and retrieval system, without written permission from the author, except for the inclusion of brief quotations in a review.

All stories in this book have been adopted by the author from stories provided by family and friends and casual acquaintances.

Although the author and publisher have made every effort to ensure that the information in this book was correct at press time, the author and publisher do not assume and hereby disclaim any liability to any party for any loss, damage, or disruption caused by errors or omissions, whether such errors or omissions result from negligence, accident, or any other cause.

Published by Kitsap Publishing
Poulsbo, WA 98370
www.KitsapPublishing.com

CONTENTS

ACKNOWLEDGEMENTS	9
FOREWORD	11

CHAPTER 1

Before the Storm of War — 1
- The Duke and I — 3
- Amelia Slept Here (Maybe) — 6
- Under Suspicion — 7
- A Hawaii Honeymoon — 8

CHAPTER 2

Pearl Harbor and Its Aftermath — 11
- An Unwelcome Surprise — 11
- Wartime Hawaii — 21
- Internment of Japanese-Americans — 25

CHAPTER 3

The Not So Pacific, Pacific Ocean War — 29
- Canton Island — 29
- Attack on Australia — 32
- The Power of Prayer — 34
- Battle of the Coral Sea — 35
- The Battle of Midway — 36
- Early Land Battles: Bataan and Corregidor, Guadalcanal — 38
- Battle of Savo Island — 41
- Makin Island Luck — 41
- Submarine Warfare — 42
- On Land and Sea in the Western Pacific Ocean and Adak Island — 43
- Native American Code Talkers — 46
- Victory in the Pacific — 47

CHAPTER 4

Island Warfare — 49
- Guam — 49
- Kwajalein — 54

iii

Saipan 55
Tutuila Island 56

CHAPTER 5
POWs 59

CHAPTER 6
War in Europe 65
Tales from the Other Side 69
Wartime in Britain 70
The Germans Were POWs, Too 71
Horrors in Europe 72
A Kind of Justice 74

CHAPTER 7
Back in America 77
Bremerton's War Years 81
Remembrances from Vets 82
The War Hits the West Coast 85

CHAPTER 8
The War's Toll on the Japanese 89
Stranded in Tokyo 89
Fire Tornadoes Over Tokyo 91
America's Options 91
Convinced to Give Up 92
Surrender! 93

CHAPTER 9
American Medals of Honor 95

EPILOGUE 101

ABOUT THE AUTHOR 103

BIBLIOGRAPHY 105

INDEX 107

This book is dedicated to my son

Joshua Iolani

And in loving memory of my parents

Cecil H. Keeler, 1902–1994
Mary S. Keeler, 1911–1999

part of America's Greatest Generation,
witnesses to:

World War I
The Spanish Flu Pandemic
The Great Depression
World War II

ACKNOWLEDGEMENTS

First, I am most grateful to those that have entrusted me with their stories of action, luck, loss, humor, and terror retold in this collection. My appreciation largely includes my neighbor, Larry Raymond, for providing me the many adventures of his father in the US Navy and to my good friend, Mike Porter, who told me about similar exciting adventures of his civilian parents. For his much-needed advice for this first-time author, an emphatic "thank you" to friend, neighbor, author, and retired US Coast Guard officer, David Martyn, also to long-time friend Christie Adams for her early advice on publishing and volunteering her father's wartime exploits, to Norma Sax for her capable editing, and my wife Susan for her patience and encouragement.

I am also indebted for the easily accessible, detailed, and succinct World War II accounts included in the online source, *Wikipedia*, and a few others, that I periodically accessed for helpful statistics, verification of content, and chronology. And then there is the computer's "spell check" function—a godsend.

Last, if there was any benefit to me to the Covid-19 pandemic, the "lockdown" isolation phase of March and April 2020 was the longed-for excuse and impetus I needed to finally start putting sixty years' worth of remembered stories and my wandering pages and scraps of notes for this collection down in pen and ink after years of procrastination—the one thing about me that improves with age.

It was mildly amusing to me that this anthology, however short and unsophisticated, modestly began to resemble a modern version of Giovanni Boccaccio's mid-1300s masterpiece, *The Decameron*, in which ten Italians fled the Black Plague and told numerous tales of love, lust, deceit, and virtue to amuse themselves in an isolated villa and pass the time as the plague ravaged the Italian countryside.

FOREWORD

Tom Brokaw's celebrated book entitled *The Greatest Generation* elevated the conscience of America. His description and examples of the American men and women who survived the Great Depression of the 1930s and went on to experience in many different roles, the rigors and the horrors of World War II, was a long-overdue and well-deserved revelation to many Americans.

This generation's sacrifices and suffering in battles were tremendous during World War II, with more than 400,000 American deaths and over 600,000 wounded. Worldwide, an estimated 20-30 million civilian and combatant souls perished. Yet, for Americans, sacrifices in everyday life, worry, and sorrow were the least. In addition to the ultimate sacrifices of the dead, the lifelong disabilities of the wounded, both physical and emotional, lasted for decades, and in many cases, for lifetimes afterward.

As their descendants and beneficiaries, we owe these Americans much of our relatively peaceful lives and prosperity. It is then appropriate that we remind ourselves of that often and honor their stories. To that end, I've tried to write about the accounts I have been given as a most modest tribute. Certainly thousands, maybe millions, of such tales have been told and recorded with great details and documentation to date, so I must plead literary innocence, as a novice writer, in the attempts that follow.

Another reason for this series of stories is to honor my deceased parents' experiences and to pass on their stories to my son. Later in life, I have learned through some bitter regrets we need to say and do important things before it's too late and avoid being haunted by words unsaid and things not done when the opportunities were right.

I included in this book a few conversations and recounted them as close as I remember what was said to me. For accountability and gratitude to my sources, the names of those who told me their stories, directly or indirectly through relatives and memoirs, are happily included as best remembered. However, at least one remains anonymous due to the nature of the two experiences recounted. Interspersed here and there, I've expanded on some background history of the events retold herein, and I've elaborated a number of times on the lives of the exciting persons involved. A few of these asides are also from my visits to specific locations that complement the personal accounts or events of the World War II experience. For the same reason, several maps are also included, giving a better spatial context to some of the stories.

As a long-time collector of postal material, I have acquired an extensive collection of artifacts from stamp dealers. So, I have also included copies of various postal envelopes from my collection that help express the times and events, as well as several photographs, one taken at a special event honoring World War II Medal of Honor recipient John D. "Bud" Hawk. I'm thankful to say the personal accounts are about survivors. Channeling the long-dead victims of World War II and their experiences would surely break our hearts.

CHAPTER 1

Before the Storm of War

By the late 1930s, the world was slowly recovering from the calamities of the early twentieth century: World War I, the post-war Spanish Flu pandemic, Prohibition (in the United States), hyperinflation and near civil war in Germany, Stalin's murderous purges in communist Russia, the excesses of the Roaring Twenties, and the resulting Great Depression.

But the specter of another war was on the horizon. Hitler and his Nazi thugs were on the move, coming to power out of Germany's post-World War I anarchy. Another egomaniac, Mussolini, had become a populist dictator in Italy. Japan was fast adding to its imperial goals, riding high in military confidence after a resounding victory in the Russo-Japanese War of 1904–05, where it ended up controlling the Korean Peninsula. It was the first Asian power to militarily defeat a western power.

A connection to this pre-World War II time was related to me by my good friend Mike Porter. I met Mike while working in American Samoa in about 1978. I fortunately ran into him and his family in Guam ten years later, both of us having taken separate postings there. Back in the States, I came to learn of his adventurous family, including his mother, Jeanne Porter (nee Long).

In 1931, Jeanne finished her BA degree in romance languages at Stanford University, at 20 years of age, and with a girlfriend, then went on a "grand tour" of Europe. As Jeanne was also fluent in German, their travels took them to Germany for a while to experience Munich. There, in a fast recovering and relatively happier post-World War I Germany, they met and actually socialized with Nazi officials, certainly many of whom later became SS and possibly Gestapo officers. I gather at the time she found them fairly decent people, years before Hitler and the Nazi party turned them into homicidal and genocidal psychopaths. Jeanne also related to her son Mike that one day she was standing on a corner sidewalk and a big car (almost surely a long, black Mercedes limousine) with Hitler in it almost ran her over as it turned the corner. Thankfully, she wasn't the first American casualty of the Nazis.

Figure 1: German 1937 postcard with Nazi Swastika and Italian Fascist Emblem (From Ancient Roman Symbol of Legal Authority)

During my sixteen years of workday ferryboat commutes from Bremerton, Washington into downtown Seattle (as an active duty commissioned officer in the US Public Health Service), I met many very interesting people. One was Walter, a phone company super-technician, who eventually related some of his early life to me. He was born in pre-World War II Germany but came to America when his widowed mother married an American GI. Walter said when he was young, he touched Hitler's outstretched hand while Hitler was driving by in his motorcade. He told me this after I first shook hands with him! Later I had my son meet and shake hands with Walter too, and I told him later "Just deal with it." Another episode of young Walter during World War II is included in Chapter 6.

Figure 2: Swastikas on US Mail! 1935 US letter commemorating US visit of German Light Cruiser KARLSRUHE

The Duke and I

In 1936, Britain's King George V (a grandson of Queen Victoria), died and his eldest son was proclaimed King Edward VIII. Edward was not seriously interested in his kingly duties, and his plan to marry the divorced and remarried American, Mrs. Wallis Warfield Simpson, was scandalous to the royal family. Edward had to go. Under pressure, on December 10, 1936, Edward officially abdicated and his younger brother was proclaimed King George VI (Queen Elizabeth II's father). The year 1936 then became "The Year of Three Kings," the first in England's 900-year monarchy. Edward was then "promoted" by his brother to the title of Duke of Windsor (marrying Wallis Warfield in 1937 after her second divorce), now living in France and getting a bit cozy in his limited British diplomatic duties with Herr Hitler. When France fell to the Nazis in 1940, the Duke and Duchess moved to neutral Spain just before a Nazi plot to kidnap Edward was implemented. (Hitler planned to have Edward returned to the British throne as a puppet king when Germany invaded Britain.) Winston Churchill soon after appointed Edward as governor of the Bahama Islands, where he remained for the balance of World War II.

After the war, the Duke and Duchess of Windsor lived comfortable lives, traveling frequently. In 1958, as a ten-year-old, I met the duke! He was the only ex-king of England. (Although, that title might include King James II of the 1600s.) At that time, one summer I was visiting my grandmother, Miriam Frances Louise Bawden Stanley, originally from Cornwall, England), who lived in Long Beach, California. When she and some visiting relatives read that the Duke was staying at the Beverly Hills Hilton, we all just had to dress up and go meet him. As luck would have it, we pulled up in the car just as the Duke was outside by himself, walking his three small dogs. I remember one was named "Davy Crockett." During our short visit, he was dressed immaculately and acted very graciously. I'm certain it was a high point in my grandmother's life, and only many years later did I realize the importance of the man—that occasion being one of the few claims to a very limited touch with "fame" in my life. Yes, finally a personal connection to the Duke and World War II.

Figure 3: 1958 Photo, author's grandmother, Miriam Stanley, the Duke of Windsor, and the author as a child (Author's Collection)

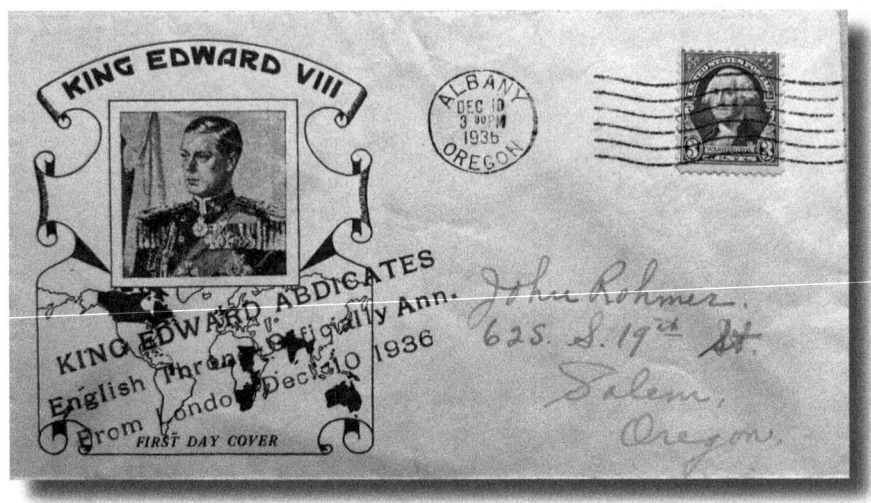

Figure 4: 1936 US letter with cachet noting abdication of King Edward VIII, with world map showing why "The Sun Never Sets Upon the English Empire" (Author's Collection)

Amelia Slept Here (Maybe)

About 1989, on an assignment to the government of Guam, my family and I visited a colleague stationed in Saipan, another one of the Mariana Islands, about 125 miles north. He gave us a great tour (which we'll hear more about in Chapter 5) that included the concrete ruins of a Japanese hospital from its occupation of the Northern Mariana Islands after World War I. It was unimpressive, small and mostly destroyed; however, it had some historical significance. Local legend had it that the famous American aviatrix, Amelia Earhart, was held there for a period by the Japanese. According to legend, she supposedly survived her plane crash on July 2, 1937, somewhere in the Pacific Ocean, on her around-the-world flight attempt with navigator, Fred Noonan. Of course to this day, nothing has been absolutely proven about a specific crash site, believed to be somewhere around Howland Island (her destination at the time) or their ultimate death or execution by the Japanese as spies. The last known "discovery" was in 2019 when bones found on isolated Nikumaroro Island were determined later by forensic analysis that could have been those of Earhart's.

Her disappearance remains one of history's unsolved mysteries, despite it being something of an American cottage industry of research and, so far, numerous inconclusive Pacific Ocean expeditions.

Figure 5: 1938 US letter commemorating the disappearance of Amelia Earhart (Author's Collection)

Under Suspicion

From friends of my Hawaii years, brothers Alvin, Sam, and Nolan Higa, comes an inspiring saga of their father, Thomas Taro Higa, born in 1916. He was a Hawaii *nisei* ("second generation" in Japanese) in a family that had emigrated from the island of Okinawa, far south of mainland Japan. They settled on the windward side of Oahu, and when he was young, he and two older siblings were sent back to Okinawa to live with relatives and to be educated. Early on, Higa was fascinated by electricity. After years of living and schooling in Okinawa (that would serve him well in World War II and then having various jobs in Osaka), in 1937 he started university studies and began working on inventions and potential US patents. But his frequent visits to the American embassy regarding routine citizen checks and his patent applications appeared suspicious to Japanese officials, and he was accused of being an American spy. After being roughly interrogated by Japanese authorities in 1939, he decided to return to Hawaii and help with the family farm. Here he set up electrical generation for his family's farm using spare car parts to assemble a turbine in a nearby stream, a unique achievement at the time for a rural household far off the electrical grid.

When war was looking increasingly inevitable in the US, his earlier ties to Japan identified Higa to US Army investigators as a possible Japanese sympathizer. He was then, even pre-war, "drafted" under an irregular process into the all Japanese-American 100th Battalion of the US Army. Higa and his unit were subjected to a whole year of Army basic training, first in Wisconsin and then in Mississippi. Higa's story in World War II picks up later in Chapters 6 and 8.

A Hawaii Honeymoon

On another, very personal level, pre-World War II had a significant event for me. My father, Cecil Keeler, born 1902, was from a little gold-mining town, La Grange, in the western foothills of the Sierra Nevada Mountains in California. He spent most of the Depression years in the San Francisco Bay area; but in 1935, a generous and lonely ex-ladyfriend sent him a ticket on an ocean liner to join her in Hawaii—a gift he couldn't refuse. In 1940, my mother, Mary Stanley, from the US east coast, was recruited as a charge nurse to come to Hawaii's premier medical facility, Queen's Hospital in Honolulu. They were married October 23, 1941, in Honolulu, and then honeymooned on the island of Kauai, 80 miles north of Honolulu. They came back to start what they expected to be a happy life in Honolulu—not far away from the tranquil Pearl Harbor Navy Base.

Figure 6: Author's father, Cecil Keeler, Hawaii skindiver and spear fisherman, 1935 to 1950 (Author's Collection)

Figure 7: 1935 US letter postmarted upon USS ARIZONA (BB39) (Author's Collection)

CHAPTER 2

Pearl Harbor and Its Aftermath

An Unwelcome Surprise

On an otherwise peaceful Hawaiian Sunday morning, December 7, 1941, the world changed. Just before 8:00 that morning, the American naval base at Pearl Harbor outside Honolulu suffered a pre-emptive surprise attack by the naval forces of Imperial Japan. A number of smaller US bases on the island of Oahu were simultaneously attacked: Army bases Schofield Barracks, Fort Ruger (at Diamond Head), and Fort Shafter, army airfields Hickam and Wheeler, and the air stations at Kaneohe and Bellows on the other side of the island.

American casualties were over 2,400 dead and 1,000 wounded, along with huge losses of Navy ships (more than twenty damaged or destroyed, including eight battleships), and many aircraft and support facilities. The next day in Washington, D.C., the US Congress declared war on Japan by a vote of 388 to 1.

Germany and Italy declared war on America days later, followed by American declarations of war against them, all reminiscent of the "falling dominos" war declarations of World War I after the Sarajevo assassination in 1914.

Japan's earlier declaration of war, intended to be delivered to the US State Department on December 7, immediately prior to the attack, was bungled in D.C. by the Japanese diplomatic staff and delayed.

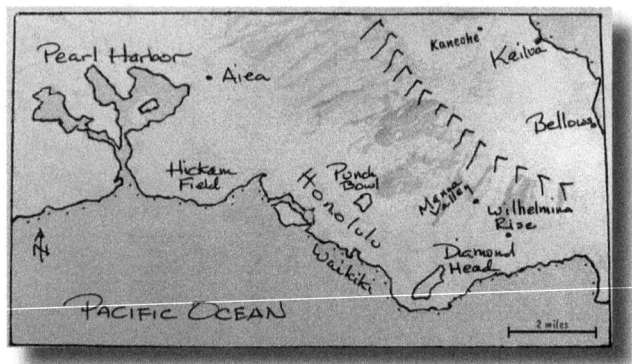

Figure 8: Map of Honolulu

Had it been timely delivered, hopefully the "surprise" attack element may have been reduced with immediate notifications to Hawaii's military bases, with hopefully much less carnage and loss resulting.

But now America was formally and totally engaged in the two-year-old war started on September 1, 1939, when Germany invaded Poland, although Japan had invaded China in 1937. It was now another world war—truly global this time. Volumes have been written about fascinating aspects of pre-war strategies, events, warning signs that the reader is encouraged to investigate; but here begins our many assorted tragic and sometimes humorous stories of just some of the less famous combatants, victims, and observers of this war, among many millions.

Jeanne Porter, previously dodging Hitler's personal motorcade in early 1930s Munich, had since married engineer Jacob Porter and by 1941 had twin boys—my good friend Michael and his brother Jackson. On November 6, 1941, Jacob had put Jeanne and the boys on the SS MATSONIA ocean liner to Honolulu to live there while he was employed on Canton Island, 1,800 miles southwest of Honolulu. Here, he was to oversee a runway extension project to completion and they could relocate to his next runway job in his contract. (Canton Island had no natural water source and it was not recommended that families live there.)

Figure 9: Jacob and Jeanne Porter with two-year-old twin sons Michael and Jackson arriving in Honolulu 1941 (Porter Family Photo)

About a week later, the family was reunited in Honolulu for a few days before Jacob took off on a Clipper flight to Canton Island. Jeanne and a new friend, socialite Gay, then had several weeks of gracious mingling with Honolulu society. They met Duke Kahanamoku, two-time swimming gold-medalist in Olympic competition and famous surfer. They located a rental house for the family, all the while Jeanne feeling that even a short living stint in Honolulu with the twins was going to be wonderful. She found a furnished home on the outer slopes of the celebrated Diamond Head crater, now an exclusive residential area, and the family settled in, until that fateful December 7 Sunday morning.

With bombs and strafing devastating Pearl Harbor, Jeanne realized that Japan was attacking, especially when overhead an American B-17 bomber coming in from the US mainland was shot down by two Japanese Zero fighter planes, and a Japanese bomb landed on the nearby Queen Liliuokalani School, where the family was directed to go in an emergency. (Liliuokalani was the last monarch of the Kingdom of Hawaii; deposed in 1898 by American businessmen, aided by the convenient presence of a detachment of US Marines.)

With excited neighbors confirming a real state of war existed, however unofficial as yet, Jeanne packed up the twins, a few precious items, and a supply of baby food, and drove off to her friend Gay's house in Manoa Valley, where they felt a bit safer. From the radio, they heard the order for an immediate blackout of all buildings and after dealing with the whole upsetting situation for a while, with a possible Japanese invasion to follow, Jeanne and Gay had "stiff bourbon and coca colas" and fell asleep.

In the morning, Jeanne, somewhat confused, borrowed Gay's shovel and buried much of the boys' baby food and her silverware in the yard. Jeanne also related one of the few humorous events of that day: In the evening, on one of the mountainsides behind the city, there was a blinking light that the police investigated. After a strenuous climb, they found a woman milking a cow, with the cow's tail waving across the lantern the lady brought up the hill.

Jeanne and the twins later returned to the US West Coast and reunited with Jacob only after his wartime duties were over. More on Jacob Porter's war experiences in Chapter 3.

Early that fateful morning, my parents, living on Liloa Rise in lower Manoa Valley at the time, took a phone call from my dad's bother, Jack Keeler, also living in Honolulu. He said he and his wife, Olga, were having an early morning breakfast in Waikiki, and "they were being strafed by Japanese warplanes; the radio said Pearl Harbor was also under attack!" My folks then hurriedly dressed and ran a few blocks down the street to an overlook, likely above Punahou School and, indeed, watched the continued aerial bombardment and hours of destruction at Pearl Harbor in the distance to the west. Unfortunately, I never asked about their lives right after that, although I do recall them mentioning the immediate fear, then and thereafter for a long time, about a possible imminent Japanese invasion and a brutal occupation. This was shared by everyone in Hawaii until the decisive American victory in the north Pacific's Battle of Midway in June 1942, and the earlier "encouraging" Battle of the Coral Sea in May 1942, in the southwest Pacific.

The American fleet out at sea near Midway Island sunk four Japanese aircraft carriers that had been part of the six-carrier fleet involved in the Pearl Harbor attack, for great strategic and national satisfaction. This is considered the vital turning point of World War II's Pacific theater. Had Japan won the battle, they had intended to take Midway Island, defended by US Marines, and then attack Hawaii again, as well as Fiji and Samoa.

Almost as surprising as the initial Japanese attack were two events, related by an account of Frances Leth, given to me by Keith Marzan, a son of good friends of my parents. The Leth family lived up high on Wilhelmina Rise behind Diamond Head and had a commanding view of all Honolulu and out west beyond Pearl Harbor.

At about five o'clock a.m. on the day of the attack, Frances witnessed newly arriving US warplanes from the West Coast and in the direction of Pearl Harbor that were shot down, not having properly identified themselves. The next day, American guns from Fort Ruger, emplaced and hidden in the slopes of Diamond Head, once again were shooting at arriving US planes, similarly not identified. Obviously, some fatal screwups.

Frances Leth, like Jeanne Porter, told of a near-fatal event that occurred that historic Sunday afternoon. Boy Scouts, wearing white shirts, were spotted on the hills behind the city and were thought to be parachutes of landing Japanese forces. Although shot at, none were hurt. The scouts and their leader were understandably not quite prepared for that day's many events when they left early that morning.

My father once told me a story he heard through the war's local unofficial channels of a Japanese plane leaving the Pearl Harbor attack that got damaged and eventually crash-landed on the small Hawaiian island of Niihau, just west of the island of Kauai. (Niihau is unique—it is privately owned and reserved for only full-blooded Hawaiians.)

When the Japanese plane crashed, a large Hawaiian fellow, eventually identified as Kanahele, went to investigate and help if needed but was unaware of the morning's attack on Oahu. The Japanese pilot, Shigenori Nishikaichi, survived the crash and shot the approaching Hawaiian twice but did not kill him. Surprised and then incensed that he was shot for trying to help, he killed the pilot with his bare hands. This led to the saying at the time, "Don't shoot a Hawaiian; you'll make him mad."

But like many of the war's incidents, several years later more detailed information emerged about this story. Still without news on Niihau of the attack, the surviving pilot on Niihau soon confided in the lone Japanese resident of the island what had happened and convinced him to retrieve the pilot's handgun, which had been confiscated, and to steal a shotgun. Before long the duo sort of ran amok on the island until the evening of December 12, when they were cornered and the now-wounded Kanahele killed the local Japanese turncoat, forcing the pilot to commit suicide. Kanahele was later honored with several military awards. The seditious action of the local Japanese fellow (citizenship uncertain) was also considered in the American government's eventual decision to enact the internment of the US West Coast Japanese communities.

Despite carefully researched advanced plans of the Japanese Navy and its fliers, one very important strategic American military installation was unknown to the enemy and not touched in the attack. Years before, some far-sighted military planner recommended and got approval for a huge underground fuel storage facility two and one-half miles inland from Pearl Harbor, close to Aiea. It was still under construction at the time of the attack, but in total secrecy inside Red Hill, as it was known, and would eventually contain a total of 250 million gallons of fuel within its twenty steel tanks, each measuring 250 feet tall and encased in concrete. No doubt this facility greatly aided the military's efforts in the busy days and years afterwards.

Besides fuel facilities not destroyed, another tactical failure of the Japanese raid was missing the three US aircraft carriers out on maneuvers (more on that shortly). But having many of the Navy personnel away and safe on leave in Honolulu that Sunday morning was a mixed blessing, as more staffing onboard may have helped some to defend the ships but may have increased casualties. Another fortunate failure of the attack was omitting attacks on Pearl Harbor's drydocks, later absolutely vital in repairing many of the damaged ships.

The next day was understandably full of continued damage control, care for the casualties, and top-level emergency meetings on immediate military and civilian response. But there was one more military action to be faced that day. A Japanese midget (aka mini) submarine had run "aground" on the reef at the Bellows Airfield on the other side of the island from Honolulu. Five of these two-man subs with two torpedoes each were involved in the Pearl Harbor attack. One was sunk inside the harbor and one outside the harbor, the latter the result of the first Japanese-American action of the war when a US patrol boat fired upon the surfacing sub and sank it early on the morning of the main attack. Two other Japanese subs were never accounted for, but a downed pilot made his way onto Ewa Beach, west of Pearl Harbor, where he was killed in a small arms shoot-out with responding US Army troops—the first US/Japan land combat of the war.

For the sub ashore at Bellows, likely something went very wrong with its navigation, there being no shipping on that side of the island. An army motor pool unit from Fort Shafter that included my Uncle Jack was quickly sent with some troops to secure and recover it. When they arrived, the Japanese officer in charge of the sub was captured and the body of the junior officer was found later in the nearby surf. Most interestingly, many years after hearing that story from my uncle, I had a chance encounter with an old man in a wheelchair that brought up another aspect to that recovery operation that day.

It seems this gentleman was one of the Marines sent along on that mission, and he had a fascinating piece of information: The junior officer's death wasn't by drowning—he was a victim of foul play. But it hasn't ever been divulged if his death was from an attack or possibly from *seppuku* (Japanese ritual suicide by disembowelment).

The historical accounts I've read just mentioned the junior officer had drowned after abandoning the sub, but I rather believe this witness's story.

This midget sub (see photo) was repaired and later toured around the US to promote World War II war bond purchases. On the big Navy base at Apra Harbor, Guam, in the late 1980s, I saw another such sub placed on a long, elevated pedestal in remembrance of the simultaneous Japanese attack on Guam. From later research, I learned it was reported that before launching, all the midget sub crew members were issued swords and pistols, indicating the missions were expected to be eventually fatal in execution or in failure.

Figure 10: The Japanese "Type A" midget submarine HA-19 hauled up on Bellows Beach. National Archives and Records Administration, cataloged under the National Archives Identifier (NAID) 295996.

Figure 11: Historical Marker at Bellows Beach, (Author's photo)

A retired US submariner with Hawaii connections once told me that his uncle in Honolulu was a taxi driver, and the day after the attack, he and all the other taxi drivers in Honolulu were "instructed" to report to Pearl Harbor and nearby Hickam Field. They were to carry all the dead bodies away to some central morgue of sorts. It was probably a pretty unpleasant day for these civilians, now witnessing the attack's carnage, upfront and very personal in the backseats and trunks of their cars. Many of those killed at Pearl Harbor are laid to rest inside an extinct volcanic crater, "Punchbowl", in the middle of Honolulu, now called the Memorial Park of the Pacific. (On the slopes of this crater, much later I attended Robert Louis Stevenson Intermediate School, 1962-63.)

One day, while I mentioned my work on this collection, my neighbor, Larry Raymond, volunteered an interesting written account by his father, Richard "Dick" R. Raymond, a sailor in World War II with the Navy rating of gunner's mate. Stationed on the heavy cruiser, USS ASTORIA, the elder Raymond left on his ship from Pearl Harbor on December 5 to escort the US aircraft carriers USS ENTERPRISE, LEXINGTON, and the SARATOGA out to sea for maneuvers and target practice. Raymond writes in his memoirs that all the ships had only target ammunition, and if they had been caught by the Japanese at sea, they would have been dead ducks, not to mention having these carriers caught tied up at Pearl Harbor and most certainly lost. But thank God, these three carriers survived and two of them were vital in the US victory later in the Battle of Midway, although the USS LEXINGTON was sunk the month before in the Battle of the Coral Sea.

Richard then recounted that upon docking in Pearl Harbor some days after the attack, the ship's propellers stirred up many decomposing bodies and body parts from the earlier attack. He said the visual scene was disturbing enough, but the stench was just horrible. What a visceral memory to have.

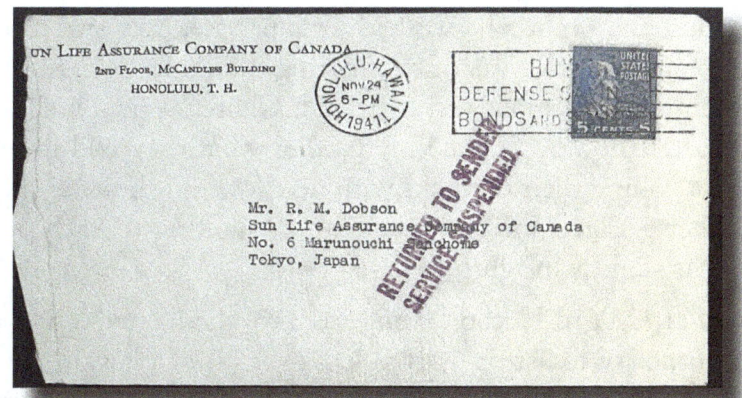

Figure 12: Prophetic message on November 1941 returned letter to Japan (Author's collection)

Figure 13: Letter postmarked during the Japanese surprise attack on Pearl Harbor (Author's collection)

Wartime Hawaii

In the ensuing days, my mother was offered a commission as an Army nurse, but as a newlywed, she declined. Not long after, she became a mail censor for the military, rising to a supervisory position. Later, during or after the war, she returned to nursing in

Honolulu and eventually worked for a private, exclusive medical clinic. She once told me of vaccinating a famous heiress, Doris, and her equally famous actress friend, Claire, at the clinic, most likely after the war. I asked my mother what they said to her as she was poking their buttocks with needles, and she said, "Nothing. They ignored me and just went on talking to each other." That was slightly insightful.

Soon after Pearl Harbor, Congress gave the United States military authority to assert martial law over all of Hawaii. Curfew and blackout periods were typically 6 p.m. to 6 a.m. Everyone was fingerprinted and given ID cards that had to be carried at all times. Inoculations for typhoid, smallpox, and diphtheria were likewise mandatory. Alarm sirens were constructed, and block wardens would check houses for required buckets filled with sand, bathtubs filled with water, and assurance that all residents knew where to turn off water, gas, and electric services in emergencies. The block wardens patrolled the neighborhoods, diligently enforcing blackouts.

Violators and those suspected of various crimes went before Army judges, without juries. Both Frances Leth and my father confirmed that even before you saw a judge, you were required to give a unit of blood! Some recent reading about "military justice" in war-time Hawaii yielded that sometime after the war, the US Supreme Court ruled all martial law convictions of civilians in Hawaii during the war were improper and they were all overturned. However, nothing I read said anything about reparations for the "donated" blood and possible days in an Army stockade.

Civil defense efforts were organized in all locations. Lloyd Kawahara, father of my good friends from my school days in Hawaii, Elvis Kawahara and his brother, thus found himself stationed on the Hamakua coast of the Big Island of Hawaii as a coastal guard, with a shotgun and three shells. He later joined the famous, second-generation *nisei* Japanese-American 442nd Army Regimental Combat Team as a medic.

My father, born in 1902, was too young for World War I service and exempt from the draft in World War II, so during the war, he served as an Army labor investigator on Oahu, looking into unexcused absences in critical wartime industries and support activities, tracking down some malingerers at the beach, maybe. He said one time his investigation took him to an illegal cock fight in the jungle attended by a crowd of Filipinos. They rapidly disappeared back into the jungle upon seeing him, leaving all the betting money, that my Dad didn't touch.

News in Hawaii was highly censored in case of enemy spies and off-shore monitoring of broadcasts by Japanese submarines. One night in the middle of the war, many Honolulu residents heard a loud explosion, with no following official mention or explanation. Via an informed friend a few days later, my father found out a Japanese plane dropped a bomb on a hillside in back of the city. Just a few years ago, I finally read about it—the bomb exploded on Makiki Heights, just behind Roosevelt High School, that I was to attend much later, 1963-66. The plane was catapult-launched by a submarine off the island, but it seems the wartime blackouts were successful enough.

Two other important wartime events were also hushed up but related to my father through friends. On one night at one of the island's military bases, a black/white race riot broke out in a barracks (or possibly between segregated barracks) and only ended when one of the rioters got hold of a serious weapon and slaughtered much of the other side. Again, nothing officially mentioned. Another story was my father witnessing a large number of ammunition and supply ships that were anchored in the West Loch of Pearl Harbor blowing up in a horrible, one-after-another conflagration. Again, not a word in the news, but again many years later I read a confirmation where this accident sunk nine ships, killed 163, injured 346, and damaged twenty buildings on shore.

Rationing was also in place, similar to the mainland US, especially since almost everything had to be shipped to Hawaii, and civilian staples were then at the expense of important military items. One thing rationed was illustrated by a humorous tale of my father's: One day he was returning home from the north shore of Oahu after fishing, when he passed a car on the side of the road. Up the road a bit, he picked up a clean-cut young man, and he asked him if that was his car back there and what was the problem. The fellow said he had serious engine problems, whereupon my Dad ventured, "You're a Navy pilot, aren't you?" Surprised, the young man said, "Yes, but how did you know?" Dad replied, "We know you pilots are always secretly cutting your gas with Navy aviation fuel, and if you're not careful, you fellows blow up your car engines!"

The large number of people of Japanese ancestry in Hawaii at that time were first and second generation, *issei and nisei*, and this presented the military authorities a unique situation after Pearl Harbor. However, because they were overwhelmingly loyal US citizens and held many of the professional and skilled jobs in Hawaii considered vital to maintaining functioning and effective sectors of Hawaii's civilian and military economies, the forthcoming infamous Executive Order 9066 by the President giving the US Army population relocation powers, couldn't practically be applied to the islands. But a number of Hawaii Japanese, certainly many that were still Japanese nationals, were quickly taken into custody as suspected spies, as were a few Japanese-Americans who were reported as speaking openly with pro-Japan sentiment. These few were placed into the Honouliuli Internment Camp outside Honolulu. (They were later to include some POWs.)

The maternal grandfather of my Hawaii friend, Kazuo Shirakawa, owned the Okabayashi Store in Kaneohe, Oahu, and was quickly interned in the Honouliuli Camp soon after the Pearl Harbor attack. He had worked at one time for the Japanese Consulate General (presumably in Hawaii) and was well-known as a leader in the local Japanese community. To pass the time while interned, he skillfully hand-carved numerous wooden models of various things, patriotically but ironically, including US airplanes and warships, a few of which carvings his grandson has inherited and appreciates as his only connection to him. When Okabayashi's wife became very ill, he was released to care for her and reopen his grocery/mercantile store to serve his rural community.

Interned somewhere in the US southwest, the paternal grandfather of another Hawaii friend, Raymond Maeda, had been eventually picked up and interned after reports of his frequent pro-Japan war conversations in his Honolulu neighborhood. But his son, Ralph Maeda, had a special security clearance because he was in charge of alcohol production at the California Packing Corporation's pineapple packing plant (later to become Del Monte). This trust in many Japanese-Americans who held jobs in Hawaii was not unusual, but some prejudicial wartime regulations still existed.

My dad told me some beaches were sometimes close to Hawaii's Japanese population. Apparently, it was thought that secret messages could be sent from these locations to offshore enemy submarines. But knowing how important fresh fish was to the Japanese culture and diet, when Dad had a good day doing his ocean free-diving (no SCUBA for years to come) and spearfishing on his way home, he would stop by his Japanese friends' homes and share his catch with them. He was a kind soul, and I always enjoyed little stories I'd hear from others about him doing thoughtful, generous acts throughout his life. (Dad told me once he was the second owner of the first pair of swim fins in Hawaii and had to make his own glass dive googles. I remember seeing these fins as a child—heavy, hard rubber, and not at all flexible. Dad was also a fishing partner of Duke Kahanamoku, later to be Sheriff of Honolulu for many years.)

Internment of Japanese-Americans

I once asked my other friend with the interned maternal grandfather if he had any interesting World War II stories from his father that he'd like to share, and he just said, "He fought for Japan." Nothing more volunteered, nothing more asked on that occasion until much later (Chapter 8). At a summer job I had while attending the University of Hawaii, a middle-aged Japanese woman in Honolulu once told me that when she was a kid during the war, none of the other children of Japanese ancestry she played with wanted to be the enemy when they played war. These Hawaii *issei and nisei* generations were loyal Americans, no doubt the same as those on the American mainland.

Unfortunately, most of the mainland Japanese-Americans didn't enjoy the same trust as their Hawaii counterparts and were subject to internment if they lived within 200 miles of the West Coast, as so many did. The entire national internment project remains highly debatable in its intent and execution. Some of those Japanese nationals (non-US citizens) caught up in the post-Pearl Harbor hysteria were eventually repatriated to Japan (see Chapter 5 for one such operation). Others may have had different outcomes. It is worth noting that in World Wars I and II, many Americans of Italian and German ancestry were also interned. My father actually witnessed this happening to an older German couple farming in rural California during World War I, when he was working for them as a teenager during a harvest. Their very vocal sentiments to the harvesting crew were strongly anti-American.

In Hawaii, by the third day after the Japanese attack, 482 Japanese, German, and Italians were taken into custody by US authorities. Of these, 43 were US citizens. Ultimately, an estimated 2,000 Japanese from Hawaii were interned, for a total of about 120,000 Japanese-Americans interned in the US during WWII. (In Hawaii, a more respectful term used is "Americans of Japanese Ancestry").

In a bitter and sweet event, our earlier mentioned Porter Family in Honolulu (mother Jeanne and her twin two-year-old sons, Mike and Jack) were finally being returned to the US mainland in October 1942, aboard a converted German ship, believed to have been captured earlier in the war. This ship was part of a much larger convoy and it carried US civilians being repatriated, as well as a group of Hawaii Japanese headed for internment camps. Years later, Mike's mother told the twins about the voyage and that the toddlers seemed to roam at will onboard, given the slightest "opportunity," and they happily mingled frequently with the Japanese passengers providing some welcomed innocent interaction and entertainment of sorts. Mike remembers his mother telling them that upon boarding, she was admonished by the ship's captain that if anyone on the voyage (such as her kids) were to fall overboard, the convoy would not stop for any rescue, or any other reason!

Interestingly, another civilian source, Maedene Lum (nee Liu), was also on a similar Navy convoy Hawaii to SF as a seven-year-old girl with her mother that year, and the ship had a teenage Japanese girl either fall or jump overboard. The convoy (of seven large ships and 12 Navy destroyer escorts) slowed and launched a rescue mission...unfortunately unsuccessful. The normal five-day transit would usually take nine days due to defensive zig-zag courses. Passengers on the converted luxury civilian liner, the SS LURLINE, now painted battle grey, were required to wear dark clothes, pants only for women--no skirts allowed, and assemble at 5:30 am each day on deck to perform drills--donning life jackets and practice boarding life boats. While the decks were cold and windy, Maedene remembers how nice the Navy staff was offering hot cocoa those mornings and allowing the kids to bring blankets outside to stay warm.

About 2002, a friend of mine was hired for a project to document the internment experience of local Japanese-Americans on nearby Bainbridge Island. Now a popular Seattle suburb served by frequent ferry boat crossings. We visited two internment camps in California: Tule Lake in the far north with its iconic/ironic guard tower and dilapidated barracks, known for its less-cooperative "guests," and the well-known Manzanar ("apple orchard" in Spanish) camp much further south on the high-desert, eastern flank of the Sierra Nevada Mountains, that included Mt. Whitney at a 14,505-foot elevation. Not much remained in *Manzanar* except a stone guard house at the gate and the gym, now a museum/interpretive center. But the more adventurous visitor can still find several abandoned, boulder-lined, now dry waterfalls and pools built by the internees—some peace and cultural comfort for those harsh years. Closer to the mountains, there is a simple, but elegant, Japanese-themed memorial that was built years later to honor the internees.

CHAPTER 3

The Not So Pacific, Pacific Ocean War

Soon after the surprise attack on Pearl Harbor, the Japanese also bombed US forces on other Pacific Islands: Midway Island (the furthest northwest island in the Hawaiian chain), Wake Island (2,300 miles west of Honolulu), Guam, and the Philippines. The Japanese also invaded all but Midway days after.

Canton Island

On remote Canton Island, 1,800 miles southwest of Honolulu, jointly administered by the US and Britain, there was a contingent of US civilians working with military construction personnel. Since November 1941 they were constructing a runway extension to better serve increasing American aircraft flights crossing the Pacific, and for the planned use of US bombers (one of many clues that the United States was expecting war with Japan sooner or later). Upon hearing of the Pearl Harbor attack followed by the other attacks, this group was concerned that it wouldn't be long before Japan also attacked them on Canton Island. On December 10 the call came to evacuate all civilians from the island.

There swiftly followed preparations to gather provisions for a group of 111 civilian workers and a few family members, and three days later they left on two tugboats, the MV MAMO and the MV MONTEREY, pulling a 300-ton barge with its human cargo. This group included my good friend's father and leader of the civilian contractor, Jacob Porter, (mentioned in Chapter 2), and coincidentally, Roland "Red" Haack, a great-uncle of another friend of mine, Julie Weiss. They set off for the closest American base, the US Navy base in Pago Pago Harbor on the main American Samoa island of Tutuila, a "scant" 1,000 miles to the south and arrived there on December 19 without incident in transit.

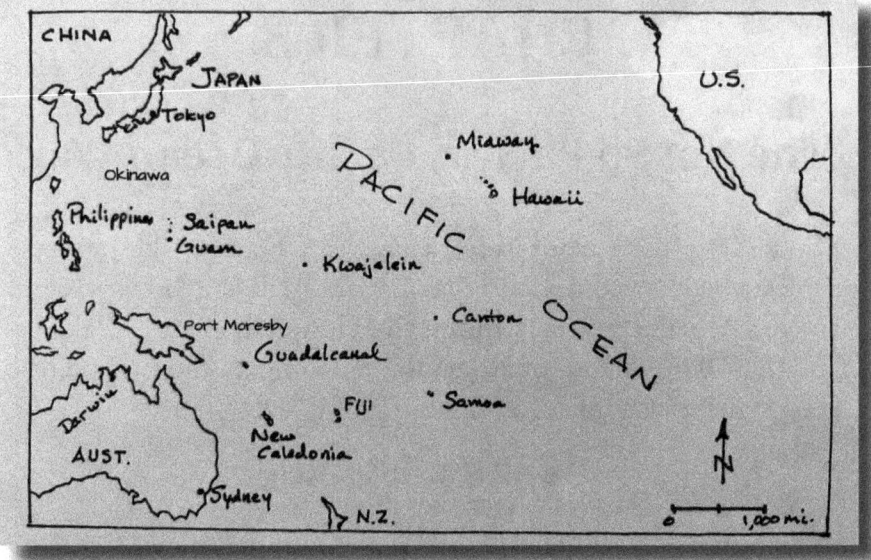

Figure 14: Map of the Pacific Ocean

However, upon entering Pago Pago Harbor, this small flotilla was met with serious suspicion from the Navy base commandant and upon their disembarking, he ordered them all placed in a stockade for more than a day-and-a-half without food. It seems this officer, after being told by an observer that two Japanese battleships and a carrier were headed into the harbor, was thereafter not reasonable to deal with. (I am not sure how that little flotilla could have been so badly mischaracterized—maybe too much *kava*, a South Pacific Island ceremonial drink considered psychoactive.)

Eventually, the Canton Island refugee party was freed and remained on Tutuila Island until January 2, when just the actual workers departed on the Hawaiian inter-island ship, SS HALEAKALA, for New Caledonia. On January 10, they arrived in the capitol, Nouméa, to find their company, Hawaiian Constructors, had not arranged for any of the equipment and supplies needed for the New Caledonia runway construction project, nor was there any expectation of such for months to come. Apparently, the Pearl Harbor attack and new war-footing had disrupted all sorts of American communication and shipping around the Pacific. Two days later, the group was dropped off in Nepoui Bay, closer to the runway work site, with just the clothes on their back and a two-day supply of food.

Being quite the driving, charismatic leader and negotiator, Jacob Porter soon convinced the local public works agency of the strategic importance of his project and got it to lend him the needed construction equipment for the work. (The island's government was ineffective, as it was divided by loyalties to the Free French resistance and the German-controlled, Vichy French government and would not commit to the helping the American-led project.) Then working with the local village leaders, he received other supplies and assistance, including somehow getting inmates of a local prison to be freed if they agreed to help with the construction—and with pay. These wages and cash for fuel and other supplies for this project were now being financed by an unusual source—winnings from Porter's weekly big stakes poker games with the wealthy local French landowners! Later and much further away, he referred to this as the "fleecing of the French."

With the necessary equipment, supplies, crew, and a group of happy convict laborers, a new 5,000-foot runway was completed in thirty-four days, in time for a fleet of American B-17 bombers to land. Before he left, Porter's grateful and now liberated and proud convicts carried him ceremoniously on a made-up throne through the streets of Nouméa. Porter's ride back to Honolulu was in a B-17 bomber, where he was allowed to practice firing a .50 caliber machine gun in the belly turret since they were short a gunner. (Jacob Porter was quite the multitalented character, working at one time as head of the US Works Project Administration of the San Francisco area, employing 25,000 workers, and frequently holding high profile poker parties with celebrities and business leaders at San Francisco's prestigious Olympic Club. He had many other adventures during and after the war.)

Attack on Australia

To protect its newly invaded interests in Indonesia, Japan in February 1943, attacked Darwin and its strategic harbor on the northwestern coast of Australia. Two-hundred forty-two Japanese aircraft, launched from carriers, bombed ships in Darwin's harbor and two nearby airfields of the Royal Australian Air Force. The attack killed and wounded hundreds and destroyed ships and planes that Japan was worried would be used to thwart its imminent invasions of Java and Timor islands to the northwest. Fortunately, Darwin was never attacked again during the rest of the war.

I visited Darwin in about 1989, while stationed in Guam, flying down on a US Air Force tanker plane accompanying B-52s on a training mission. The city was rebuilt and modern, but hotter than blazes—about 100 degrees F and nearly 100% humidity, being only about twelve degrees south of the equator. Talking to locals there, I heard several times a popular story about a suspected Japanese submarine during the war, spotted by radar in the harbor. After it was "neutralized" by harbor defense guns, it was discovered to be a BIG ocean-going crocodile, called a "salty" Down Under. (Having visited a croc farm on that trip, I can attest to how huge these monsters really could get. One crocodile I saw was, in circumference, about the linked arm-spans of two men. The salties, sharks, sea snakes, and deadly jellyfish in the waters of much of Australia make beach swimming there less recreational and more of a survival challenge.)

Again from the northern reaches of Australia, comes another story, related by my good friend Michael Porter, about his one-time personal physician, back in California after the war, Robert Harmon, MD, when he was a P51 Mustang fighter pilot during the war. At the time, Harmon was flying reconnaissance and cargo support flights for the Eleventh Air Force out of an Australian base on Cape York, one of the two northern "horns" of the continent. While there, he developed a very fond taste for Foster's Beer, an Aussie dietary staple. He would regularly carry as much of it on his flights as his cockpit would allow, cooling nicely at high altitude, for a celebration and reward for a landing—something always worth celebrating, of course. But on one flight over the Torres Strait, one of his two spent Mullin auxiliary fuel tanks wouldn't release. Despite Harmon trying several quick aerial maneuvers to dislodge the fuel tank it still wouldn't fall away. This situation posed a serious hazard, especially if aerial combat was suddenly necessary, so Harmon needed to descend and land fast to get rid of it.

At that point, a runway at strategic Port Moresby on Papua-New Guinea Island was closest, but as Harmon approached, he found it was still under construction with equipment and workers all over the developing runway. Despite being waved off by two red flags, he felt he had no choice and made a dramatic but successful landing. He was immediately rushed by an angry, sweating Navy Seabees crew with their commanding officer. Harmon was threatened with all sorts of punishment, including a court martial and imprisonment, possibly after a severe beating on the spot. Harmon, ever the resourceful, quick-thinking, and good-natured fellow, then calmly began handing out his bottles of chilled Foster's Beer to pass around to these guys who had been in the hot, tropical sun for hours that day and not having tasted any decent alcohol for who knows how long. Well, after some serious quaffs, those cold beers smoothed things over big-time, and before long the offending fuel tank was removed and he was good to go, likely with an admonition not to do that again until the runway was complete, when he was then…VERY welcome to land again. Harmon, for his preparedness, could have been a Boy Scout icon.

Elsewhere in Australia during the war, another adventure took place. My neighbor, Geoffrey Meredyth, (the only other Geoffrey I've ever met in person), told me of a Japanese attack in Sydney

Harbor during the war when he was very young. His memories were still vivid of hiding under a kitchen table with his mother the night of May 31, 1942, while hearing tremendous explosions in the nearby harbor. Apparently three Japanese midget subs attempted to torpedo the American heavy cruiser, USS CHICAGO, in the harbor. One sub was caught in the harbor's submarine netting, but one got through and fired two torpedoes, none of which hit the cruiser, but which did hit the Australian ship, HMAS KUTTABUL, killing twenty-one on board. The fearsome explosions that Meredyth and his mother heard were depth charges going off in the harbor, eventually sinking the sub. The third sub was found later, scuttled on the shore outside the harbor. According to Meredyth, all the surviving Japanese sub personnel committed suicide, but were given full military honors during burial, which really upset Sydney's population!

The Power of Prayer

On the Malaysian peninsula, about 2,000 miles west/northwest of Australia comes a tale with a strange twist, from an elderly Chinese woman known as Popor, told to her modern, seasonal neighbors in Malaysia, my friends Stephen and Ina Inklebarger. In December 1941, Japanese forces landed in several Indochina locations, one being northern Malaysia, intending to take the British island-fortress of Singapore to the far south. Being well-defended on the water sides, the Japanese were to march south in secret over many miles of primitive jungle roads and attack it from the land at the tip of the peninsula, erroneously thought to be impossible. To prevent advance warning of the southerly march, Japanese scouts cut any lines of communication found along the way and murdered all inhabitants along the route, which would have included this Chinese lady (as a child) and her family. But as recounted to the Inklebargers, at her parents' house along the way, the Japanese witnessed her and her family at prayer in the house's Buddhist shrine, and just left without even a word of warning. She is still so grateful that for whatever reason they weren't killed and were left alone, not that life under Japanese control for the rest of the war was pleasant.

Battle of the Coral Sea

Also in May 1942, a large flotilla of Japanese ships, including aircraft carriers, sailed south intending to attack and occupy strategic locations on the island of Papua-New Guinea. But it was challenged and turned back by a group of American and Australian warships and carriers in the Coral Sea. The battle was something of a stand-off but was considered the Allies' first "victory" in the Pacific, restoring confidence in America's naval might. It was the first naval battle in history where carrier-launched planes were the only weapons used upon each side's ships.

Again, Richard Raymond was aboard the USS ASTORIA and participated in this battle, successfully gunning down several attacking enemy planes. During the battle, the USS LEXINGTON was sunk, and Richard helped rescue many of those survivors. After the battle, he said they stayed in the Coral Sea for 101 days, existing on fewer and fewer rice and coffee rations, three times a day. But upon returning to Pearl Harbor, their dietary sacrifice was rewarded with a serious, dock-side feast by Navy Command. Soon after that, off they sailed again to another fateful engagement.

Figure 15: Letter from the carrier USS LEXINGTON (Author's Collection)

The Battle of Midway

This naval battle was one of the greatest and most important battles in the Pacific. Fought in June 1942, US planes sank four of the six Japanese carriers that participated in the Pearl Harbor raid and seriously impaired Japan's naval capabilities for the rest of the war. Without that victory, the balance of World War II Pacific warfare may have been considerably different in specific outcomes, although it is thought an Allied war victory was inevitable. Again, Richard Raymond kept his gunnery skills honed and brought down more Japanese attack planes but suffered a bullet in his leg. Not stopped for long, he said he worked it out, kept the bullet as a souvenir and went on firing. (Apparently, Raymond was a determined character. In his childhood, he once took a venomous water moccasin snake to school and dropped it onto his classroom floor to watch the panicked reactions. Later on when reporting to his first Navy ship assignment, he tried to bring a donkey onboard as a mascot.)

Figure 16: Likely a Marine's letter (passed by a censor) mailed prior to the Battle of Midway, June 4-7th 1942 (Author's Collection)

Figure 17: Letter mailed from carrier USS YORKTOWN with special photo cachet of the ship. Severely damaged in the Battle of Midway, it sank several days later. (Author's Collection)

Early Land Battles: Bataan and Corregidor, Guadalcanal

In April 1942, Japanese land forces attacked US and Filipino forces on the Bataan Peninsula, north of Manila, with superior numbers and air support and soon after forced a surrender with the infamous, deadly Bataan Death March begun shortly thereafter. Under a hot sun, 76,000 Allied POWs were marched for sixty miles without food or water to a new Japanese prison camp. An estimated 5,000 of the 12,000 Americans captured died of thirst or were executed along the way. At a dinner party once, I met a Filipina-American and eventually asked her about her older relatives' World War II experiences in the Philippines. She simply said her father survived the Bataan Death March—nothing more needed to be asked.

Figure 18: First Day Cover celebrating the 3-Cent "Win the War" stamp with photo of General Douglas MacArthur and a map of the SW Pacific War Theater. (Author's Collection)

Figure 19: 1942 Envelope from Japanese Occupation of the Philippines (Author's Collection)

Later in 1942, much further south in the Pacific there was the long-running, bloody battle on land and sea around the island of Guadalcanal in the Solomon Islands, not ending until February 1943. At a ninetieth birthday party in 2006 for my neighbor, Peter Strom, I met an even older friend of his, name forgotten, with a chilling tale of his infantry time on Guadalcanal. Many of us younger folks have heard about those terrible battles, and after I acknowledged the ugly conditions of rain and mud, with mosquitos, malaria, snipers, and venomous snakes taking their toll, he said "But the worst was the Japanese troops and their *banzai* (roughly equivalent to "long life" in Japanese) charges out of the jungle every second or third night. Those ended up in the dark—fighting hand-to-hand—to the death. I still have nightmares about it." And his wife spoke up saying, "I still can't sleep with him, he's too violent." To this very day, I've never been able to forget that impression of such savagery and the constant expectation of that terror in the Americans fighting there.

That bloody experience was later also testified to by another good friend in Hawaii, Christie Adams, whose father, Henry Jackson Adams, Jr., also fought in Guadalcanal and six other Pacific island battles, including Tulagi, Peleliu, and Okinawa. He eventually suffered emotionally, becoming a troubled alcoholic. Prior to the war, Adams was a championship shooter and was the Stanford University rifle team captain 1928-1930. After graduation he became a California policeman, later being a deputy sheriff in San Diego and then being hired by the FBI in 1940, seeming to make a successful specialty of capturing bank robbers in New Jersey. In 1935, Adams won both the prestigious Dupont and Harrison trophies, as the best all-around rifle and pistol marksman in America.

In April 1942, Adams was commissioned as a lieutenant and was hand-picked to join the First Marine Raider Battalion, one of America's early modern elite special forces. After specialized commando training in Samoa, he employed his superb shooting skills as a leader in reconnaissance and combat, killing an estimated 200+ Japanese enemy during the war, many at up to 300 yards away, and once killing fifteen enemy soldiers in a single close-quarters firefight. He also survived 75 reconnaissance flights in low/slow flying spotter planes over enemy-held islands. Once, he predicted a Japanese surprise attack for the next day that his Marines prepared for and successfully repulsed. When his commanding officer asked him how he suspected that in advance, Adams replied that the day was Emperor Hirohito's birthday (a likely auspicious day for the Japanese troops) but he remembered the date only because it was also Adams' birthday. During his three years of combat in the Pacific, he was wounded only once, in Okinawa, ironically from American antiaircraft fire, but did catch malaria at one point. During recovery from his wounds, he received a personal note from J. Edgar Hoover, Director of the FBI. Friends remarked in photos of him after the war, the younger, handsome, 6'4" Hank Adams, was noticeably a very different man.

After the war he became under-sheriff of San Diego and later rejoined the Marine Corps, eventually becoming provost marshal of the San Diego Marine base and retiring as a colonel. He passed away in 1978 and was later featured with a full chapter in the book *More of the Deadliest Men Who Ever Lived* by Paul Kirchner, in which some of the preceding details were found.

In 2017, 94-year-old Edward Wright related to me a part of his time as a Navy ship's boilermaker in the vicinity of Guadalcanal. He said one day he was waiting to board his ship, the USS TUTUILA, when he witnessed an explosion of a nearby Navy ship, the USS SERPENS, manned largely by US Coast Guard personnel. The explosion completely destroyed the ship as it was carrying munitions, and all hands were lost, amounting to the single largest loss of US Coast Guard personnel in World War II.

Battle of Savo Island

Soon after the first invasion of Guadalcanal, there was a disastrous nighttime naval engagement (August 8–9, 1942) off nearby Savo Island, just NE of Guadalcanal. Here five Allied warships were sunk by Japanese naval forces and three others were damaged in one hour's fierce action. One of the severely damaged ships was the USS ASTORIA, with Richard Raymond still on board. He recounts the severe damage done amidst horrible human carnage with wounded sailors slowly dying on the decks and the ship on fire for days. Later, the ship rolled over so fast the survivors had to jump overboard into bloody waters where they and the dead bodies were attacked by sharks. When he and thirty-one other survivors (219 were killed or missing) were rescued and under way back to Hawaii, Raymond couldn't sleep, nor go below deck, and he hung onto several lifejackets for days. It sounded like that naval battle and its aftermath were the equivalent of the horrible ground fighting on Guadalcanal.

Makin Island Luck

As World War II raged on, US forces invaded more previously Japanese-held Pacific islands, including Adak Island (August 1942) and Attu (May 1943) in the Aleutian Islands, Tarawa and Makin Islands (November 1943) in the Gilbert Islands, and Kwajalein (February 1944) in the Marshall Islands. On Makin Island, Elmer Hart, US Navy, formerly a young farmer from Moscow, Idaho, served as a medic and on-board his ship, sometimes as a baker. He told me of his tremendous luck on Makin Island, when twice, Japanese hand grenades landed very close to him, but neither of them went off. He later served in the bloody battles for Saipan (June 1944) and Okinawa (June 1945), no doubt saving many lives.

Submarine Warfare

Meanwhile, America's submarines increased in numbers under the Pacific Ocean and increasingly sank Japanese warships and cargo freighters. John Yacko, US Navy, enlisted for submarine service in 1943 right after completing eleventh grade in Philadelphia. After several patrols in the South China Sea rescuing downed Allied pilots and sinking their share of enemy ships, his skipper once went "up periscope," unaware of two Japanese destroyers nearby and suddenly saw depth charges in the air (called "hedgehogs" by the US). Submerging rapidly, the crew endured and gratefully survived three hours of continuous pounding by Japanese depth charges. Another time on a practice dive (thank goodness), the top hatch to the sub wouldn't close, and by the time it resurfaced, three or four feet of seawater had collected in the sub's lowest level.

Once off the coast of Vietnam, Yacko's sub skipper planned a shore attack to blow up a train tunnel on the coast but called it off at the last moment. Another time his sub was strafed by American planes because the sub didn't respond to the right "IFF"—military radio term for " Identification, Friend or Foe?" Yacko said he believed that most of the sub commanders were reckless, but he felt the Navy seemed to encourage that. Somewhere I remember an account of another American sub that successfully attacked numerous coastal targets on the northern islands of Japan itself with covert shore landings, placing explosives, and paddling swiftly back to the sub. When these exploits were eventually made known, the sub and its crew became real war celebrities back home.

Regarding sub adventures, our peripatetic Richard Raymond, returning from the Battle of Midway in a small boat inside Pearl Harbor itself, had quite a time. Next to his boat a Japanese sub's periscope, having snuck in behind his ship and the sub nets, came up and Raymond grabbed it. As the two vessels parted, he ended up in the water and swam to a buoy, followed soon by an American PT boat and a float plane aircraft starting to drop depth charges on the sub. The sub was sunk, but Raymond remembers the close-by concussions and riding that buoy several times ten to fifteen feet in the air as the depth charges went off. That would be memorable.

On Land and Sea in the Western Pacific Ocean and Adak Island

Much further west the Allied invasion of the Philippine Islands was being undertaken, led by US Army General MacArthur, fulfilling his promise "I shall return," after escaping the Bataan battlefield for Australia in 1942.

After supporting the various Philippine island assaults, Navy Task Force 38, consisting of about eighty-five warships and supply vessels, headed back east to refuel at sea. In the middle of this always tricky operation, a typhoon (a hurricane, later named "Cobra") came up and took the fleet by surprise on December 18, 1944. Huge waves and fierce winds pummeled the fleet and two days later the toll was staggering—three ships lost, twenty-nine ships damaged, 146 aircraft damaged or swept overboard, and 790 sailors dead or missing in the seas. Only 94 sailors were eventually rescued. Edward Wright was aboard one of the ships and related to me that 90-foot waves had pushed his ship at times into extreme lists, close to what they feared would be "rollover" status. The task force's commander, Admiral Halsey, was officially blamed for the disaster, but was not punished. Six months later in

June 1945, Halsey's fleet was again battered by another typhoon, "Viper," but without serious losses. Learning from these events, the Navy quickly set up serious weather stations all over the Pacific to prevent future catastrophes at sea.

In 1943, a second-generation American of Dutch descent, Tony Roozen of Minnesota, graduated from US Army Officer Candidate School and in 1944 was involved in the Battle of Leyte Island, close to the center of the Philippine Archipelago. Serving as a Battalion Communications Officer, and after four amphibious combat landings and successive battles on Mindoro, Luzon, Mindanao, and Davao islands, Roozen felt he had "marched up and back down" the Philippines by the time Japan surrendered in August 1945. Once, he had to run about 500 feet under intense motar fire to retrieve a Jeep and then pick up his crew and escape. He was awarded the Army's Bronze Star for that. He remembered later on the sadness he felt as a Battalion Executive Officer, seeing so many young platoon leaders being killed so soon after taking their first command in the field.

Roozen said he had a Japanese sword (see photo), a Japanese flag, and a bad case of malaria as souvenirs of his Philippine adventures. From the malaria, he was in sick bay on board all the way back to Seattle, where he recovered well-enough for a celebration on the town but relapsed and was unconscious for days on a train going back to Wisconsin. He retired from the Army in 1971 and moved back to Washington State where I met him years later.

Figure 20: Anthony "Tony" Roozen, Lt. Col. US Army (retired), with souvenier Japanese sword (Author's Photo)

About midway through the war, Peter "Pete" Strom, who was then a policeman in Wisconsin and much later became my neighbor, was enticed into the US Coast Guard, being offered an E-5 rating over a competing Navy E-4 rating.

His first and last assignment was on Adak Island in Alaska's Aleutian Island chain, where the almost constant wind, rain, and cold were new and unpleasant to him, despite experiencing many an upper Midwest frigid blizzard while growing up. It seems his police background and the base's location were intended for a fast response to the anticipated surrender and occupation of Japan. For some reason, that never materialized for his unit. As a civilian, he took a job transfer to Bremerton in Washington state, where he and his family settled into a house in about 1947, next door to where I would eventually live.

(I digress here a bit with some memorable episodes about Pete, a full-blooded, second-generation Norwegian living in Wisconsin, never learning English until he had to start school. Growing up, he did ski jumping and worked in a store as a teenager, when one day his boss asked him to bring in some refreshments to the back room for some visitors. There he was introduced to some well-dressed men, Alphonse "Al" Capone and some of his associates. Years later, Strom was playing football as a 200-lb. lineman at a teacher's college in La Crosse, Wisconsin. For two summers, the team scrimmaged with another Wisconsin football team practicing nearby—the Green Bay Packers! Strom had a very eclectic life and passed away in 2015 at 99 years old. He was a long-time member of the Sons of Norway and a respected member of the Elks, Masons, and Shriner fraternities.)

Native American Code Talkers

In the years 1984-87, I was assigned to the Navajo Area Indian Health Service in Window Rock, Arizona, where I was frequently reminded of the important role of the bilingual Native Americans who provided vital, secure radio transmissions to our forces fighting in World War II. On the reservation there, the Navajo Code Talkers were considered royalty, those living and those having passed away by then. It was riveting to learn more about them and the other tribes that participated. Besides conversing in the Navajo (the "Dineh" as they call themselves) language, which was already almost incomprehensible to listening enemies, the messages were further in code using Navajo words to identify various objects and persons. Examples were calling a tank a "badger" in Navajo, a submarine an "iron fish," a destroyer a "shark", or my favorite, Hitler as "crazy white man." Without a doubt, these Native American combat radiomen helped tremendously in the US war effort in the Pacific and in Europe.

Quite a few of these radiomen (certainly at least in pairs) were also recruited from other American Indian tribes such as the Assiniboine, Cherokee, Cree, Comanche, Mohawk, and Tlingit (from Alaska). But surprisingly, the practice originated in World War I, and Germany, pre-World War II, sent teams of German linguists to the United States to learn Native American languages, anticipating using this technique in the war to come. Fortunately, the languages were too numerous and difficult. American forces also used Basque and Welch bilingual troops, but in only carefully selected situations, as pockets of these speakers were in other locations around the world.

Figure 21: Censored 1943 letter with photo celebrating US Navy "Seabees" (Author's Collection)

Victory in the Pacific

After months of vicious land fighting and aerial *kamikaze* plane attacks of the US fleet off the coast of Okinawa, the invasion and occupation of Okinawa was over in June 1945. (*Kamikaze* in Japanese meant "divine wind" after the two typhoons that wrecked Kublai Khan's successive Mongol invading fleets off the coast of southern Japan in 1274 and 1281.) This most costly, last big battle in the Pacific resulted in 12,000 American troops killed, but Okinawa was crucial to plans for the continued aerial bombing of

Japan and was going to be the staging point for the future invasion of the home islands of the enemy.

Finally, in 1945, atomic bombs were dropped in Japan on August 6 and 9 on, respectively, Hiroshima and Nagasaki. The Hiroshima bomb, code named 'Little Boy' was delivered in the American B-29 bomber, Enola Gay, taking off from Tinian Island in the Northern Mariana Islands. On August 14 Japan agreed to an unconditional surrender, and on the USS MISSOURI battleship, September 2, 1945, a formal surrender ceremony was held in Tokyo Bay. The war against Japan was over, ending World War II. Germany had surrendered earlier on May 8. President Franklin D. Roosevelt had died April 12, 1945, and was succeeded by Vice President Harry Truman.

Among many thousands of now unneeded US servicemen and women being "mustered out" was our good friend (by now) Richard Raymond. Leaving from the Navy's Treasure Island base in San Francisco Bay, he hitchhiked rides from truckers heading east. Helping to drive the trucks, he made it back to his parents' home in Worcester, Massachusetts very quickly. When he arrived one night unannounced, one by one he shocked his mother, sister, brother, and finally his father with incredible relief and joy. After his ship went down with few survivors in the Battle of Savo Island and they had not received any of his subsequent messages sent back home, they assumed he was dead. Raymond recounts a most happy and tearful homecoming that night.

CHAPTER 4

Island Warfare

I've chosen to include some World War II stories specific to these islands as a separate chapter for the most complicated reason that—I've been to them. I've lived and worked on the islands of Guam and Tutuila (the main island of American Samoa) for a total of five years. I've visited Saipan (the main island of currently, the US Commonwealth of the Northern Mariana Islands) and Kwajalein (largest island of the eponymous atoll, belonging to the Republic of the Marshall Islands), where I once had a stopover on a space-available military flight across the Pacific.

Guam

The Japanese aerial raid on the US Territory of Guam, December 8, 1941 (same date as December 7 back in Hawaii), was focused on the US Navy shipping in and on US aircraft stationed at an airfield at Guam's Apra Harbor. (Guam had been a US spoil of war since the 1898 Spanish-American War.) Two days later the island, roughly about thirty miles long by about five miles wide, was invaded and occupied by Japanese land forces. The American forces, mostly Navy, were quickly overwhelmed, and those not killed during the bombing or in defense mostly surrendered. Several US servicemen, however, escaped and made their way into Guam's jungles and hills. One of these was George R. Tweed, a survivor staying free, barely, until the US forces invaded Guam on July 21, 1944. Much later he wrote a book about it, *Robinson*

Crusoe, USN. Many of the local Chamorro people hid him and others, but many paid with their lives, when the Japanese learned of it.

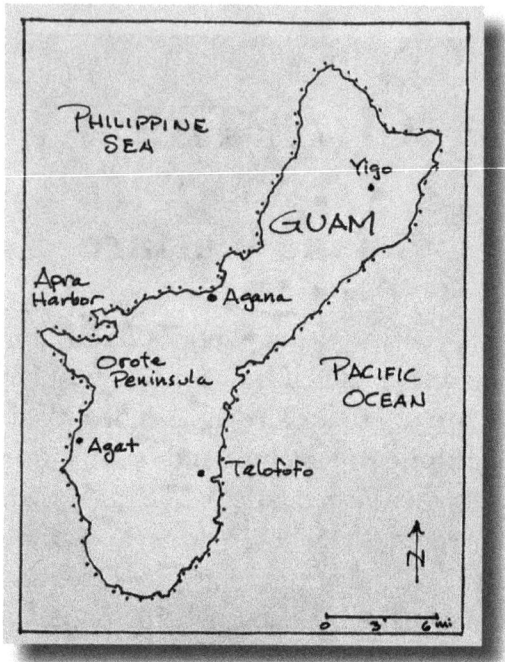

Figure 22: Map of Guam

As few, if any, of the Guam Chamorros spoke or understood the Japanese language, some of their bilingual, distant cousins from Saipan up north were soon imported. Saipan had been under Japanese control since the League of Nations mandated the formerly German Northern Mariana Islands be administered by Japan following World War I. After twenty years of occupation, many of the local Chamorros on Saipan had become fluent in the Japanese language and many even intermarried. While working for the local Guam utility, I did learn, while it wasn't publicly discussed, that there was still strong resentment toward those Saipan relatives, mostly among the older Guamanians who remembered the cruel conditions of Japan's occupation, usually administered by their Japanese-speaking cousins from the north.

In the Guam utility I was assigned from 1987 to 1990, in our water supply and wastewater facilities construction projects, and in other construction excavations on the island, it was very common, perhaps monthly, for contractors to come across unexploded World War II bombs that quickly had whole neighborhoods evacuated. Well-experienced Navy ordinance disposal teams would be called to expertly dispose of them. Other war artifacts were also periodically found. One that our wastewater director, David Damien, personally took me to see was in Yigo (pronounced 'Gigo') up north close to the last Japanese stronghold of the war. It was kind of surprising and a little whimsical. At the bottom of a deep sewer cut of maybe twenty-five feet deep, was an old car body—to this day still a head scratcher, but certainly a victim of the war! (Another oddity, but unrelated, was an entire bicycle we found at the bottom of an old sewer manhole—one never knew what could be flushed down a toilet there—or anywhere. Every few years, the wet wells in our sewer pumping stations had to be cleaned out, and it was like Christmas for the staff, waiting to see what would come up—expensive rings, coins, etc. that would pay for the year's office fiestas.)

Back much further south on the island, was a popular swimming/diving area called the "Piti Bomb Holes." These were typically 20-feet diameter, underwater craters from the US naval bombardment of Guam prior to the amphibious assault, starting July 21, 1944, now celebrated as "Liberation Day" on Guam. That and two other Roman Catholic church holidays were also Guam government holidays, so working for a local utility gave me three days off in addition to all US federal holidays that I, of course "reluctantly" observed, a typical relaxed life out in the islands.

Even after the war, Japanese soldiers were still being captured in the jungles of Guam. Prior to Japan's final battle in the north, a number of Japanese troops were ordered to disperse and conduct continued guerilla warfare from the jungles. Many of these surrendered on order of the Japanese Emperor Hirohito that was broadcast on September 4, 1945. Before and after that, the US command authorized a local Chamorro group called the "Guam Combat Patrol" that, surely with revenge in mind, hunted down and killed 117 of the remaining Japanese troops (Guampedia, "Japanese Stragglers on Guam"). Still, several remained and the last, Sgt. Shoichi Yokoi, was captured twenty-seven years later in the remote Talofofo area in 1972. This fellow had real survival skills. He died back in Japan in 1997 at age eighty-two.

My favorite Guam war story came in 1984 from a fellow in western New Mexico, Les Hadden, who sold us our house in Gallup. Toward the close of the war, Hadden was a civilian hired by the US Navy to direct the reconstruction of the Apra Harbor breakwater on Guam. One evening he had a dinner date with a US military nurse staying in the women's quarters on the reconstructed Navy base on the Orote Peninsula bordering Apra Harbor. When he checked in at the barracks, he was met by a big MP who first checked his ID and then issued him, even as a civilian (ready for this?), a belted holster and a loaded sidearm, likely a .45 Automatic Colt Pistol. Hadden was shocked and said there shouldn't be any Japanese to worry about at their dinner. The MP then said "It's not them…there are 30,000 horny US troops still here. It's to protect her from those guys. You bring her back safe!" I gather dinner that night went fine—no dead or wounded GI Romeos were reported.

One of the most vivid memories I had in Guam was soon after we moved there, playing cards with my son one evening while Typhoon Lynne was howling outside—and we experienced a sharp earthquake. I thought, what were the odds of that happening? In the morning it was all over, except going outside and looking at the jungle across the street. It looked like those World War II photos after a huge shore bombardment of any one of the Pacific islands, where every tree was stripped bare of its branches, and all the bushes had no leaves. The formerly lush jungle area now looked like acres of vertical sticks. We experienced about three other typhoons of consequence while there. Living in solid concrete Navy houses, including the roof, with windows rumored designed to survive coconuts at 150 mph, we managed pretty well, although the island's power supply was another thing—see next story. Most of the older, wooden houses in Guam got eventually blown down in typhoons or eaten up by the voracious local termites.

Figure 23: US letter with humorous cachet about an Army Master Sgt. (Author's Collection)

Guam suffered a post-World War II "invasion" of a nasty pest, the Brown Tree Snake. It's thought to have come here from the Soloman Islands in the many loads of rebuilding materials after the war thought to have come. Without any local predators they have reproduced and decimated most of the native birdlife, and have taken their toll on a lot of people scared to death when they unexpectedly have these creatures fall out of trees or make their way into homes. The biggest nuisance, however, is their effect on the island's electrical grid. Their incredible climbing ability gets them up almost anything, easily including the power poles where they many times decide to cross wires, getting themselves fried—and knocking out power to great swaths of Guam's neighborhoods. Small fangs in the back of their mouths are slightly venomous, but except for chewing on your fingers or hand, they were just spooky to find all over the place, especially outdoors at night. A friend's daughter once woke up in the morning with one attached to her arm. She quickly pulled it off and smashed it against the wall, being left with a nasty wound on her arm. The worst incident I heard about while there was a mother finding her baby with just a skeleton of a hand in the morning, as the attached snake's venom had dissolved the flesh overnight! Guam is working hard to keep these creatures off the power poles and to restore the native birdlife, hoping the snakes will eventually turn cannibal.

Kwajalein

When I started my new assignment in Seattle, after leaving Guam in 1990, I met a gentleman, Warren Montgomery, who was soon to retire. As we got acquainted, he related that he was a flyer in World War II, mostly ferrying aircraft back and forth over the Pacific. When he mentioned Kwajalein as one of his many stops, it piqued my interest as I had been there once for a few hours on a space-available air force cargo flight. I remember it being idyllic looking and bordering a large lagoon, with a modest collection of small buildings (concrete of course), some dormitories, many coconut palm trees swaying in the soft breezes, and all traffic being pedestrian, bicycle, or official golf carts. The base's function was to track test missiles launched from the US West Coast, splashing down (hopefully) in the middle of the adjacent huge lagoon. It likely had even more sensitive functions.

However, to Montgomery, at the end of the war, it was the remnant of a US naval bombing that killed an estimated 5,000 Japanese troops, defending the island until the end. On stopovers he stayed at the improvised bachelor officers' quarters (BOQ), but said if it had rained recently, the stench of the Japanese massgraves next door, was just horrible. Years later, I happened to meet a minister, Rev. Lawrence Burton, at a memorial service. He had quite a few stories. One was meeting a man who still was troubled by those thousands of dead Japanese bodies—he was the one that had to bulldoze them into the mass graves on the island.

Obviously not a pleasant memory to have for decades afterwards, another legacy of war.

Saipan

While we were still living in Guam, we visited a PHS engineer colleague and his family, who was stationed north up on Saipan Island. As Japan had occupied the Northern Mariana Islands, of which Saipan was the largest, for twenty years until the US invasion began June 15, 1944 (starting with two days of heavy US naval bombardment), the battle for Saipan was extremely bloody. Of the 71,000 US land forces involved, more than 3,400 were killed, and more than 10,00 were wounded. On the other hand, despite long preparations of defenses, rough terrain, and the never-surrender Japanese warrior code, "*bushido,*" when it was over, an estimated 24,000 Japanese troops lay dead with more than 5,000 suicides, many being Japanese civilians and their children jumping off mountain and sea cliffs. Unbelievable to western values, the Japanese Emperor in a radio address on July 1, had decreed that Japanese civilians that would commit suicide in the upcoming Saipan battle would be rewarded with a special spiritual status. Only about 900 Japanese lived to be taken as prisoners by the Americans.

Off the shore of the western coast of the island remains a reminder of the US amphibious assault on Saipan—a US tank, slowly rusting away in the surf. On the northern end are the ruins of the last Japanese battle HQ in a large limestone cave formation. In it, our friend's son one day found a hidden, forty-year-old diary of a Japanese soldier. He turned it over to a Japanese official there (Guam and Saipan are heavily visited by Japanese tourists), and it was repatriated to the soldier's family in Japan—likely a sad but a most appreciated occasion for the family, given one of Japan's serious traditions of ancestor respect.

(Atop Saipan's Mt. Topochau, my friend pointed out the distant home of a reclusive multimillionaire, at the time the last living founder of a well-known international delivery company.

He moved there years ago, deriving federal income tax breaks as an official resident of the US's Commonwealth of the Northern Mariana Islands, similar to Puerto Rico. My friend Stan said the multimillionaire once asked him if he would manage a Dunkin' Donuts franchise if he would buy it. Stan didn't bite.)

Off the southwestern tip of Saipan is the smaller island of Tinian, taken by the Allies on July 2, 1944. Long-planned aircraft runway improvements and lengthening were immediately undertaken. From this airfield, the Enola Gay B-52 Superfortress bomber (modified for a nuclear bomb) later took off on August 6, 1945, and delivered the atomic bomb "Little Boy" on Japan's Hiroshima City. The 12-hour roundtrip flight and bombing resulted in four square miles of total destruction and up to 80,000 dead and 70,000 injured. A second B-29 took off from Tinian on August 9 and delivered the second nuclear bomb, "Fat Man" on Nagasaki City. Surrender by a shocked Japanese Emperor and the reluctant Japanese military leaders followed before long.

Before we left Guam in 1990, I allowed our young son, Joshua, to accompany our good friend Patrick Morrissey in a small plane leaving Guam and flying 120 miles over open ocean to Tinian, where Patrick performed a classic "touch and go" landing and returned to Guam. Our faith in Patrick's piloting skills and experience was rewarded and Josh gained a unique experience on historic Tinian Island, however brief.

Tutuila Island

In 1977, with my then wife and our four-month-old son, I moved to Tutuila, the main and largest island of American Samoa, to begin work for the local territorial government. For the second time in my life (see Chapter 7 for the first), I saw the unusual name "Roggeveen." In 1722, a Dutch sea captain, Jacob Roggeveen, was the first European to "discover" the Samoa Islands. After a century of further Pacific exploration and colonization by various European Powers, the larger Samoa islands to the west came under German control, mostly for the exploitation of the abundant copra (coconut meat). The smaller group of Samoan islands to the east came under more a benevolent administration of the US, mainly looking for future military use of the deep water and well-sheltered Pago Pago Harbor in the middle of Tutuila Island. A modest US naval facility was eventually constructed in the harbor, and many years later my work office was in a dilapidated old Navy hospital building, with no air conditioning and huge rats roaming my desk drawers during the night. German Samoa was given over to New Zealand control after World War I, and in 1962, it became an independent island nation.

During the Spanish Flu pandemic of 1918–1920, American Samoa was notable as one of the few locations not affected. It seems a very progressive Navy doctor managed to enforce a strict quarantine in the harbor and prevented any cases occurring there. Interestingly, 100 years later, again due to strict preventative measures, (for visitors, advance vaccinations and negative Covid tests, and quarantine upon arrival), American Samoa had no reported Covid cases from January 2020 until September 2021, when two cases were reported, with the infected arrivals taken immediately to secure quarantine locations. (Friends who have recently returned from years in American Samoa reported during their time there, no one masked up or had to socially distance!)

During World War II, American Samoa was important as a stopover for US ships and aircraft traveling between Hawaii and battle zones in the southwest Pacific and was used for jungle combat training of US troops. Besides the landing of American workers for Canton Island refugees fleeing a possible post-Pearl Harbor attack (Chapter 3), only one real incident of World War II warfare touched American Samoa, the only US soil south of the equator. On January 11, 1942, a Japanese submarine got past the shore guns at Blunt's Point at the mouth of the harbor and surfaced further into the harbor. From their deck gun, the crew fired off two shells toward the US Navel Station Tutuila (1899-1951). One shell did some minor damage to a Navy building but the other hit and destroyed the store of the Shimasaki Family, the only Japanese family in the whole territory—quite ironic. A second source reports that 15 shots further off shore, were fired, but with the same results.

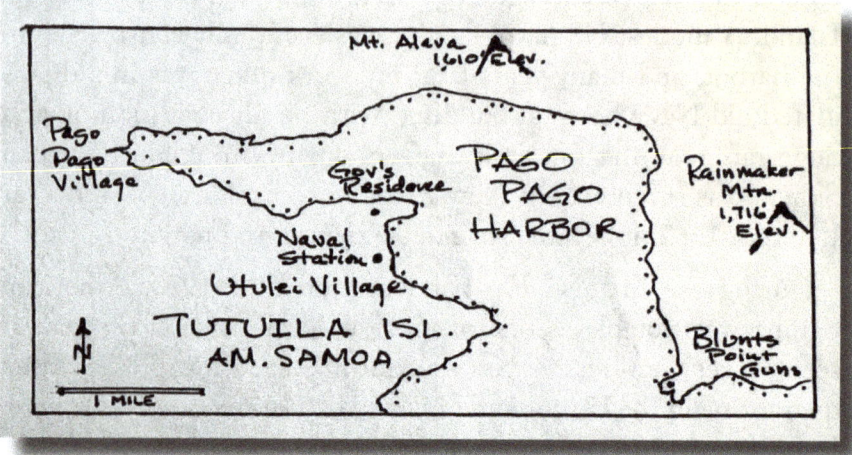

Figure 24: 1942, Pago Pago Harbor, the site of brief deck gun attack from a Japanese submarine on US Naval Station Tutuila, June 11, 1942.

My two years in Samoa were the most interesting of all my assignments. As the saying goes, "You can't make these things up." It was almost hilarious sometimes, and I would recommend a delightful satire, *Tales from the Margaret Mead Taproom*, by Nicolas von Hoffman and illustrated by Gary Trudeau, author of the famous Doonesbury cartoons. Trudeau used his Uncle Duke character as the newly-appointed gonzo governor of the territory and his side-kick, nephew Zonker, in search of the perfect tan, frequently in conference with the Minister of Marijuana. The characters dealt with a host of odd-ball Polynesian politics, culture, and personalities that were surprisingly close to the reality of life there.

CHAPTER 5

POWs

From 1977 to 1979, I worked in American Samoa implementing the territorial government's water well-drilling program on the main island of Tutuila. For a while, a gentleman named Larry Moran, formerly a well driller himself was assigned to me as my inspector. Larry was 84 years old at the time, and a little crusty, but a very welcome addition to my formerly one-man program.

After I got to know Larry pretty well, he told me of his capture by the Japanese while he was drilling wells in the Philippines. He was then thrown into a POW camp at the age of forty-eight, long enough that his health was being fairly compromised. Fortunately for him—a miracle of sorts—his wife, Priscilla, also forty-eight, had earlier been married to a wealthy German and had retained her German passport. So the Japanese prison authorities allowed her access to the POW camp as a wartime "ally" and she was able to help feed and attend to her husband. Surely few other POWs in World War II fared as well as Larry Moran.

Another aside, this time about Larry's wonderful wife, Priscilla. She was born about 1894 in Apia, on Upolu Island in Samoa (that and two other large islands, later became known as Western Samoa, and more recently as just Samoa. The smaller islands to the east later became American Samoa). Her father was an English trader, Harry Moors, and his wife was Samoan.

Before her birth, her father was a good friend to the famous Scottish author, Robert Louis Stevenson, who had moved to Samoa, spending his last years there slowly dying of tuberculosis, then called "consumption." After dinner one night with Larry and Priscilla, she lent me a special book written by her father about his friendship with Stevenson, who had become loved by the Samoans and was given the honorary Samoan name of *Tusitala*, "storyteller." The book was fascinating as a personal account of many of Stevenson's day-to-day adventures and various events. When he died, Samoans somberly carried his body to a nearby mountaintop above Apia, where he is buried with his famous epitaph, "Under the wide and starry sky...Home is the sailor from the sea and the hunter home from the hill..." The large house and lands where Stevenson lived with his family, named *Vailima* (Samoan for "five streams") has been the home of the Samoan head of state for many years now. Knowing Larry and Priscilla Moran was a once-in-a-lifetime special opportunity for me.

Several hours after Pearl Harbor was bombed, on a high holy day for the Roman Catholic Church in Guam, this island territory of the United States was attacked by the Imperial forces of Japan, first by aerial bombing and then with an invasion. The Japanese forces shortly thereafter essentially enslaved the native *Chamorro* people and were as cruel to them as they were to the populations in other lands they conquered. Many of the *Chamorros* were "assigned" to agricultural production, much of it rice.

Discipline was harsh. An example of this was related to me by a *Chamorro* lady working at the Bremerton Naval Hospital, name forgotten. Quietly, she told me of her mother during the war in Guam, forced to watch her elderly parents being beheaded for some offense, possibly being too old to work—so disturbing. It's estimated that about ten percent of the *Chamorro* population died during the Japanese occupation 1941–1944.

Some years ago, I was privileged to meet and know an older *Chamorro* gentleman, Anthony "Tony" Cruz and his Hawaiian wife, Margery. Tony was a young boy during the occupation and along with his family had to sleep nights in a shallow pit, close to where they were assigned to work cultivating rice. They covered the pit with a lattice work of branches covered with banana leaves for some protection, but it was still a horrible place to rest, given the mosquitos and frequent rains. Tony says he was sometimes used by a friendly Japanese soldier who appreciated Tony's local fishing knowledge, and Tony and his family enjoyed some of the catch for an occasional protein boost. Tony did survive the war, grew up, and later joined the US Navy, enjoying a career as a cook, and a great one, I might add. My years 1987–1990, serving on a Public Health Service (PHS) detail to Guam 's water and wastewater utility PUAG (now known as Guam Waterworks Authority), afforded me frequent and great samplings of delicious *Chamorro* dishes, and I enjoyed renewing years later, an acquaintance with the gourmet food at the happy gatherings at Tony and Marge's house in the Bremerton area. Tony, father of six wonderful grown children, passed away in 2019.

Figure 25: 1945: A now liberated POW "Tony" Cruz, with US servicemen at a beach on Guam (Cruz Family Photo)

Figure 26: 1974, Chief Petty Officer Anthony I. Cruz at Navy retirement. (Cruz Family Photo)

Years before I was assigned to Guam, I met another PHS officer, Captain Ted Ziegler (now retired) while I was living in Gallup, New Mexico, and commuting interstate to the Navajo Reservation across the border in Arizona. One day I asked Ted if he had grown up riding horses, since he had rather pronounced bow-legs. Ted patiently explained it wasn't horseback riding that gave him his legs. As a child living with his missionary parents in China, he and his family had been taken prisoner by the invading Japanese, and he suffered from nutritional deficiencies that led to soft bones and his eventual condition. Wow, who knew he had such a traumatic experience so young? Ted has always been quite the modest gentleman.

Much later when I mentioned to him I was collecting World War II stories, Ted shared with me a short write-up by his younger sister, Laura Darnell, about their POW experience in China. His family, except for his father somewhere else in China, was in the Hong Kong area when the Japanese attacked by air on

December 8, 1941. Ted, his mother and five siblings, slowly made it to the British island of Hong Kong, which held out under the bombardment for seventeen days. After their capture, they were moved around by the Japanese to various internment areas with many other of the British, American, and Dutch civilians (they called themselves the "BADs") in the captured area. They were poorly fed and suffered under strict discipline, although their treatment was not as cruel as that endured by the captured or surrendered Allied servicemen. (According to the Japanese warrior code of *bushido*, captured or surrendering soldiers were cowards for not fighting to the death and were not to be afforded any kind of respect, hence the many brutal treatments.)

In July 1942, they were taken on a Japanese ship to Lourenco Marques (now Maputo in Mozambique, Africa). There they were swapped for Japanese nationals from the US, and strangely enough, the former American POWs were secretly sorry for the exchanged Japanese having to return to Japan, now having some idea about austere Japanese wartime culture. From there they were transferred to a Swedish ship and weeks later, repatriated in New York Harbor where they appreciated seeing the Statue of Liberty after 16,000 miles at sea. My good friend Ted has since retired from the PHS and lives in Portland, Oregon.

A short POW story came from a friend of my wife, whose father was part of a Canadian flying crew, and who was shot down over Germany. In the crash, he was badly burned and not expected to live long in the German POW camp he ended up in. Fortunately for him, the camp had a Polish medical doctor interned there. The doctor successfully treated him and he recovered.

On a short cruise up the Dalmatian Coast (Greece to Croatia) with my wife in 2019, I met a lady named Gail, who told me about her father in World War II. He was an Army sharpshooter and was sent as a guard to an American POW camp in the deep south, possibly Mississippi. Here he apparently got very bored—seems the predominantly German POWs were so grateful to be safe and well-treated that no one tried to escape.

CHAPTER 6

War in Europe

The United States, of course, at this time was engaged in a two-front war. Along with stories about the conflict in the Pacific, I have been fortunate to also have been told of wartime experiences in Europe.

Figure 27: Thomas Taro Higa, US Army, veteran of European and Okinawan Campaigns. (Higa Family Photo)

After my Hawaii friends' father, Thomas Taro Higa, completed his year-long Army basic training in 1943, he and his unit were finally shipped out to North Africa. He later fought in Italy, where he was wounded in the famous battle for Monte Cassino. Post-recovery and back in combat, he was again wounded, this time returning to the United States for recuperation. He was concurrently awarded two Purple Hearts and the Army's Silver Star Medal for his actions while wounded. After his recovery, the US War Relocation Authority and the Japanese-American Citizens League recruited him to speak at many of the Japanese internment camps to help improve social and cultural relations, and to promote further Japanese-American *nisei* enlistments in the Army. Soon after, Higa had an important realization, and his story continues in Chapter 8.

Figure 28: Early Axis postcard showing Nazi, Fascist, and Japanese Forces routing British Forces in their respective war fheaters
(Author's Collection)

Mathias Klous Jr., a fellow ping-pong player at the Bremerton Senior Center, told me about his father's experiences on D-Day, June 6, 1944. On that long, deadly day, Klous Sr. was a young sailor piloting a troop landing craft onto one of the two American beachheads, designated Utah and Omaha. During that hazardous transit between ship and shore, his vessel was hit, disabled, and soon had to be abandoned. After swimming ashore, Klous

Sr. unarmed, realized that he was totally vulnerable to the German machine-gun fire, so he swam back out and was rescued by another landing craft and transported to the USS SUSAN B. ANTHONY, which stuck two German mines the next morning and began to sink. In two hours, all 2,689 personnel on board were able to transfer to nearby LSTs and then to US and British ships. (The Guinness Book of World Records lists this as the largest rescue of people ever without the loss of life.) Klous Sr., now on a British ship, wore a British Navy uniform until he was returned to US Forces several days later in Portsmouth, England.

Later, Klous ended up in the Pacific theater, hoping for better luck, but again escaped another near-disaster naval engagement. Probably hoping to never experience another brush with death at sea, he ended up in the Army Air Corps and stayed on to become a veteran of the newly created US Air Force (1947) until his retirement. His son Matthew continued the tradition of service and eventually retired as a Lt. Colonel in the US Army; unfortunately for me, he now confines his keen aggression to our ping-pong games.

Speaking of luck, my friend Jim Anderson's grandfather was blessed with a variety of it too. In the Army infantry in Europe, he was in a building with his unit and someone slammed a door, a rifle went off, and he was shot in the leg. Recuperating in a stateside hospital he later learned that his entire unit (likely a squad) was killed in subsequent combat.

At my mother-in-law's retirement home, I met a World War II Army Air Corps veteran, Jack Chunn, who first served as an anti-aircraft gunner in bombers over Europe. Later, on D-Day, he was on a ship and the next day, high up on a cliff above the beaches, then later on a half-track manning a .50 caliber machine gun.

In his air-to-air battles with German fighter planes, he was one of the first to fire at a jet plane, likely the Messerschmitt Me 262. But, Chunn said, they flew so fast that he couldn't hit them.

When Chunn finally made it through the worst of the European warfare, the US forces were told to retreat immediately to Germany (or what was left of it by then) and let the Russian forces have Czechoslovakia, where he was at the time.

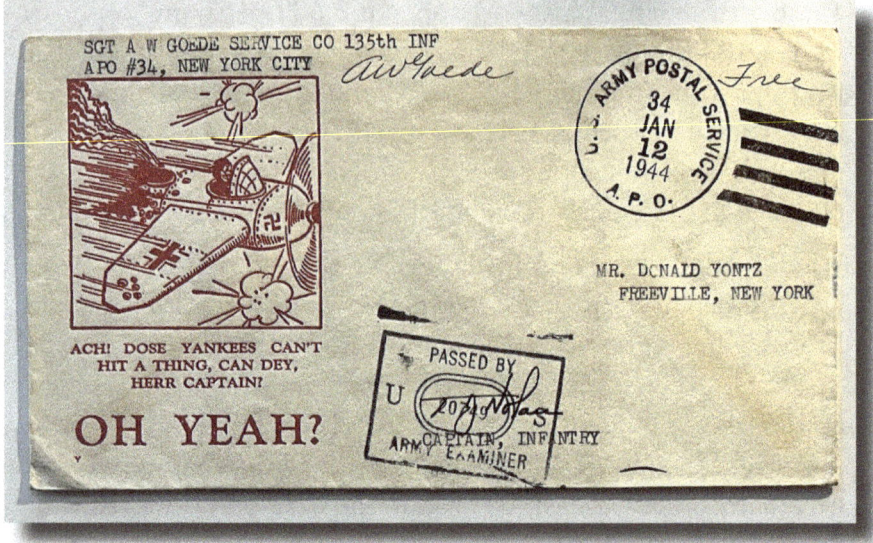

Figure 29: Censored US Soldier's mail with anti-Nazi Luftwaffe caricature (Author's Collection)

He remembers that back in Germany he was assigned to road patrols and told to pick up any refugee men without identification documents. They were almost always ex-German soldiers and were to be taken to certain farm camps where they were forced to work. Chunn was later transferred to the Pacific war theater, and when Japan soon after surrendered, for the first time he felt safe and happy to have survived the war.

Figure 30: 1942 US letter with Uncle Sam stomping on Axis leaders (Author's Collection)

Tales from the Other Side

Another lucky fellow from World War II Europe was a short, bald, stocky, middle-aged backhoe operator whom I met in 1972 on my first field visit in Puget Sound (Washington state) as a newly commissioned officer in the PHS. This fellow was introduced to me as just "Otto" by my PHS engineer colleague Murry. Otto was expertly working his backhoe on a water and sewer construction project in the old Indian community on the Swinomish Indian Reservation. The old homes were tightly packed together and Otto's extremely deft touch was indeed needed, especially when water and sewer lines had to be at least ten feet apart. Murry eventually introduced Otto to me as "the World's greatest backhoe operator" and I couldn't disagree based on my observations. Murry further explained that many years previously, Otto was a tank driver and had survived dozens of World War II tank battles where successful maneuvering was a life-or-death matter in these fierce battles. Oh, and Otto drove German Panzer tanks for Hitler. What hellish stories he could probably tell, despite his friendly grin.

My friend, Walter, told me of his resistance as a youth to US paratroopers coming down over the fields outside his German village. He and the other village boys went out with their small caliber rifles and shot at the parachuting soldiers, at least until they started to return fire. While this was a unique event to me, what he said happened next, after the troops took the village was shocking. He said the soldiers under command of their US officer went through each home looking for Nazi paraphernalia, and if they found anything, like swastika arm bands, pins, or flags, they took the adults out and executed them! Walter said he didn't witness any of it, but the grownups all talked about it, and I guess the bodies of those shot were quickly removed and buried. Over the years, I've had difficulty believing this was possible of US soldiers, but other World War II stories and rumors of this kind of treatment sadly have given this some credibility.

A related episode told to me by friend Victoria Zafft, was from her stepmother, Marianna, who was a little girl in Germany. When American soldiers first came to her town, they inspected every home. Fearful, her parents hid Marianna from the American Army troops—in their oven.

A similar tale comes from a friend of my wife's, Sonia Kunz, (nee Standaert), whose family came as refugees from Belgium after the war. As the family were farmers, the German authorities came at every harvest to confiscate most of the crops. The family was always terrified their son would be taken by the Germans to one of their notorious camps and worked to death. So in advance, they managed to hide him in a concealed compartment at the very bottom of the house's staircase with some food until the Nazis departed. Sonia's family emigrated and settled in Moses Lake, Washington, where they continued to be successful farmers.

Wartime in Britain

Once on a trip to the San Francisco bay area, a most gracious BnB host, Pamela Ferrero (nee Blacoe) related to me her wartime experience in Britain, as another young girl. Growing up in Liverpool, she remembers her parents' concern as Nazi aerial bombings took place there early in the war. They decided to evacuate her to her grandparents and their farm in rural Wales, not far away, but far enough away to be very safe. While living there, she initially went to a local school but the family believed she was picking up the "wrong" accent (speech in the UK is thought to be important to future social and employment prospects), so they changed her schooling to a more acceptable "accented" class held in the local vicarage.

Every morning her grandfather would religiously walk Pamela halfway to class, going with her as far as the local pub, where he would then join his mates until Pamela would return several hours later, and then he would walk her back home. Pamela thought her grandmother never knew of the whereabouts of her husband during those few hours each school day. But I doubt it—I haven't met a naïve grandmother yet.

Pamela eventually immigrated to Canada and then to the US, being trained and then working as a professional dietitian for many years. She also mentioned that after the war, her father was the dentist for a young Liverpudlian—Paul McCartney of later Beatles fame!

The Germans Were POWs, Too

On a much less happy note, there have been the many disturbing rumors and reports since the end of the war about the treatment of German military POWs by many of the Allied forces. An estimated 2.8 million German forces were captured or surrendered on the western front between D-Day and Germany's essential surrender in April 1945 (officially May 8). German surrendering forces numbered approximately 10,000-59,000 per day, in the period of March–April 1945. With these huge numbers of new POWs, transportation, guarding, food, and shelter for them was a major challenge for the Allies, not to mention simultaneously trying to save many more millions of European civilians from starvation. No doubt standards of humane treatment of POWs at that time had to suffer, even if no mistreatment or purposeful neglect occurred. However, still many rumors abound from that time about the extreme mistreatment of large numbers of German POWs by the US Army.

One story source that will remain anonymous admitted that once as a US Army guard on a forced POW march, he witnessed a German Waffen-SS officer harassing a lowly German soldier about carrying his gear and slowing down the march, so this American soldier just shot and killed the SS Officer, taking his Nazi SS Totenkopf ("death's head" in German) uniform insignia, with no criticism or repercussions for his actions. I gather the POW march proceeded at a better rate of speed after that. Another tale of his was earlier in combat where he was forced to shoot and presumably kill an unusual German soldier—a long-haired blonde woman in full German battle dress and armed, running towards him. That was no doubt a shock to him, but his combat experience kicked in fast enough to surely save his life. (That was a revelation to me, women in actual combat for Germany.)

Horrors in Europe

Another tale of war atrocities: a fellow, just calling himself "Frenchy," was a ping-pong player with our group for a while. He had a tale of an ugly revelation about the past war he heard as a child in America. One day he asked his French mother about a friend of hers who had no hands and visited them every few years. His mother told him the German Gestapo cut her hands off during the war as they interrogated her as a suspected member of the French resistance group, the Maquis (named after a common ground cover in France).

At a neighbor's party once, I met a Canadian gentleman, Ben Koops, who was born in the Netherlands and had two World War II stories he could remember from his childhood. The first was when Germans came to his family's house looking for any contraband. As it was, his father had just returned from bartering with a farmer-friend of his and came home with a tub of fresh butter, which, if found in the raid, would have meant prison, or execution. As the Germans entered, his mother quickly threw a towel over the tub sitting in the kitchen. Despite a thorough inspection, much to the family's great relief, the Germans never found the butter.

Again, Koops' parents and a sister escaped a near-miss wartime disaster, this time riding on a train. Suddenly a siren sounded, the train came to a screeching halt, and everyone ran off for dear life into the surrounding fields. Allied warplanes then started strafing the train, as they had sighted its rear flatbed cars carrying German cannons. Another lucky Dutch family, but then again, these stories were all from survivors.

On the outskirts of Port Angeles, Washington, there has stood a quaint French restaurant, C'est si Bon, for many years, owned and operated by an older, gracious French couple, Michele and Norbert Juhasz. My wife and I had dinner there one Bastille Day, July 14, the French National Independence Day, and enjoyed an always delicious French dinner. Afterwards, as a tradition, one of the owners would always come out after the meal and visit with the patrons; this time, after I asked about their World War II years in France, we were invited by Michele to their adjacent, quiet bar to visit and drink complimentary liquor. She told us of their backgrounds.

Michele remembered that while living in Lyon, France, she dashed with her family to a shelter, as the German Luftwaffe ("air force" in German) began bombing the city. She fondly remembered later during the city's liberation by the Allies, she and the other young girls gratefully catching sweets and chocolates in their aprons, tossed by soldiers driving through the streets. (Finally, a happy memory!) Her grandfather was a soldier in the fabled French Foreign Legion, and her father was part of the French forces in the 1939 battle and miracle of Dunkirk where an estimated 340,000 Allied troops were successfully evacuated by British naval ships, fishing boats, yachts, and merchant vessels from the French coast. (These cornered forces, saved from certain destruction or capture by the surrounding German forces, later greatly helped delay Germany from invading Britain and then helped in the successful invasion of Normandy four years later.)

Michele's husband, Norbert, was of Hungarian parents but born in northern France, close to Belgium. Before that, his father was actually a member of the famous Hussar Cavalry of World War I, fighting against the Austrian Empire. During World War II Norbert's family was removed by the Nazis to Germany as workers, but eventually Norbert escaped and fled to Austria where he lived in an abandoned car factory. After Germany's defeat and arrival of the Russians, he escaped again, this time back to France, fighting later in the vicious Algerian Civil War. When he later immigrated to America, he played violin for Hollywood movie soundtracks, where he met Michele, who had been for some time a private chef for many Hollywood celebrities (many of whose autographed photos lined the restaurant bar's wall). The couple later moved north, much to the culinary delight of many Americans and visiting Canadians in the US Pacific Northwest.

A Kind of Justice

A short memoir entitled Holocaust: Confirmation and Some Retribution by Ralph Rush, US Third Army (of General Patton fame) was given to me by my friend Keith Marzan, via one of the many family connections he seemed to have. It describes Rush's experience, after a brief firefight, of entering the first Nazi concentration camp liberated by US forces, "Ohrdruf Nord." Here, they were soon horrified to observe piles of dead bodies and the gaunt, emaciated inmates—all sickening to him and the others. The bodies included a group of still warm bodies, obviously recently executed, of allied soldier POWs.

He soon was approached by a camp inmate, a former Polish army officer, who desperately pleaded for Rush's gun to kill the sadistic camp guards that had just exchanged their uniforms for those of camp inmates, and were hiding among the others. At first hesitant, Rush eventually believed the man when the man showed Rush his Jewish ID tattoo, and gave him an earlier "liberated" German Lugar pistol and several clips of ammunition. A while later, the man, still with tears in his eyes, found Rush, returned the pistol, and thanked him profusely—long overdue, extreme justice had apparently been accomplished. About a week later, Generals Eisenhower, Bradley, and Patton visited the camp and were similarly horrified, confirming years of rumors of these camps' existence. But unfortunately, publicity of the discovery was initially somewhat limited since, on April 12th, President Roosevelt died.

A friend and retired colleague, Judy Fey, once told me about another "liberated" Lugar pistol, one that her father held in some kind of reverence. He would periodically take it out and demonstrate to Judy and her sister how it functioned and how it was to be cared for, but never explained the importance that it held for him. Her father was a member of a US Combat Engineer Battalion, not arriving in Europe until late in the war, but then doing a lot of reconnaissance, building bridges, and demolishing old fortifications. He particularly remembered a period of time in the town of Prüm, when he would give a mysterious hand stretching out from a basement window GI chocolates or cigarettes, in exchange for black market liquor or wine. In 1958, he took the family on a road trip in a Borgward Isabella car all around a much-rebuilt Europe. It was a sort of a pilgrimage for her father; that gave Judy and her sister an early appreciation of the continent's history and cultures.

In 2004 when my son was a US Air Force junior officer stationed at Mildenhall Air Force Base in central England, close to the famous university town of Cambridge, I traveled there to visit and attend his promotion ceremony. One day he took me to visit the nearby Cambridge American Cemetery, resting place of 3,812 American men and women killed in World War II over the skies of England and continental Europe. In addition to many white, marble crosses among acres of well-groomed fields, there is a long wall of 5,127 inscribed names of American personnel whose bodies have never been recovered—missing in action. On this wall I eventually located the names of Navy Lt. Joseph P. Kennedy, Jr., older brother of future president John F. Kennedy, along with the famous bandleader, Army Major Glenn Miller, who was lost on a flight over the English Channel. Lt. Kennedy was a co-pilot on a top-secret training flight in 1944, testing a heavily armed bomber that was later to be flown to the French coast and then unmanned, remotely guided into a Nazi submarine base. On this flight, something went very wrong, and the plane exploded without any trace of remains.

It was always thought that had Joseph Kennedy, Jr. survived the war, he would have been groomed for and ultimately elected US president, instead of younger brother John.

CHAPTER 7

Back in America

In writing this collection of stories, I certainly focused on tales of the warriors of World War II and admit to a shortage of personal accounts of the servicemen and women and civilians back home in America. This is indeed unfortunate, and I beg the reader's understanding. However, following are at least a few that certainly have more positive outcomes.

My wife's mother, Molly Garhart (nee Muriel State, Calbom), was born and raised in Spokane, Washington. In 1942, she was in high school and found a summer job as a messenger on the US Army's Galena Field, located about twelve miles west of Spokane. She was a classic, beautiful young blonde, and she no doubt experienced numerous advances by many of the soldiers while on her job (no doubt, some of them very crude), as the base surely had hundreds of young, unmarried soldiers. Hearing of these approaches, the older women in her dispatch office decided on a strategy to help protect Muriel and started to spread some "important news." Shortly thereafter, the word around the base's soldiers was that Muriel was…the General's Daughter. Problem solved for the rest of the summer.

After high school, Muriel attended Sacred Heart Hospital's nurses training program in Spokane and joined the US Cadet Nurse Corps, established in 1943 and put under command of the US Public Health Service. The US government paid for her tuition plus a modest living stipend and in return, required her to become an active-duty military nurse upon graduation. But close to her graduation, the war ended and the army canceled her obligations. She went on to marry a returning Army Air Force bombardier, John Calbom (who had served over Europe; first Airman on the left in the cover photo) and raise a family. She passed away in 2018 at ninety-two, mother of three, grandmother of three, great-grandmother of twelve, and my sweet and interesting mother-in-law.

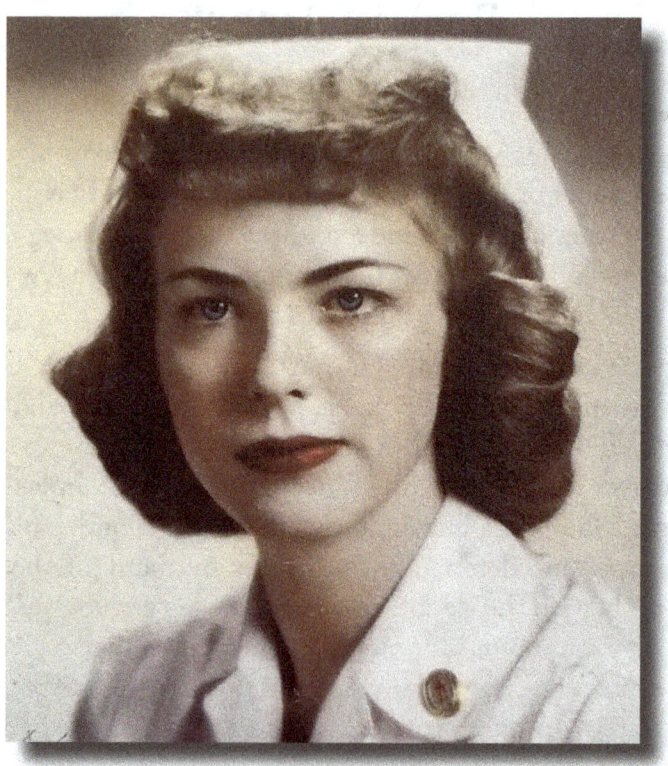

Figure 31: Muriel State, Cadet Nurse Corps, 1945
(Calbom Family Photo)

About 1992, I had the good fortune to meet an older fellow, George Meisner, and found we had a fair amount in common. He and I were both born and raised in Honolulu, graduating from the same Roosevelt High School in town, George about 1946 and myself in 1966. Much later, he and I worked separately but concurrently in American Samoa in the late 1970s. George was a consultant for only a short time, spending most of his off-duty hours at the previously mentioned "Margaret Mead Taproom" of the Rainmaker Hotel, whereas I was usually back home with my family after work. George was a "colorful" fellow—when I first met him at a dinner party, he was dressed head-to-toe in canary yellow garb. Among his many stories, he told of his popularity with his high school girlfriends in wartime Honolulu. Back then George was a volunteer ambulance driver, so he was one of a few young men with a vehicle AND permission to be out driving at night past curfew hours. He remembers the ambulance headlights covered over with black tape, except for a horizontal slit left open for minimum lighting during the night-time blackouts. I'm not sure how his dates went, but it was probably a nice opportunity for the girls to get out of the house, experience a little exciting patriotic "night-life" like applying first aid and helping to carry stretchers to the emergency room. As for romance, George never said…

Figure 32: 1944 Letter with caricature encouraging US civilian war efforts (Author's Collection)

George's career was in power generation, and he had a curious tale about running the Hilo Power Plant in 1960, on the Big Island of Hawaii. On May 23 that year, a deadly *tsunami* (Japanese for "harbor wave"), generated by a massive earthquake off the coast of South America's Chile, hit Hilo Bay—hard. Its waves funneled into downtown Hilo, destroying many of the buildings, leaving sixty-one dead, and no electrical power for miles. (The quake's wave later hit Japan, killing 180 people.) So George's still functioning power plant several miles out of town became the temporary morgue, providing refrigeration for the bodies, until identification and burial. I personally remember the *tsunami* event, as it suddenly ended my sixth grade class picnic at nearby Kailua Beach on Oahu's windward side, with warning sirens blaring and the hurried re-boarding of our buses, although no wave was later reported there. *Tsunamis* can be very selective about where they hit and how hard.

In 1972, during my last year in a graduate civil engineering program at Stanford, I applied to be and was accepted as an active-duty engineer officer in the Commissioned Corps of the US Public Health Service (PHS), one of our now eight uniformed services. The appointment was contingent of course upon graduating with an engineering degree, since my earlier BS was in physics from the University of Hawaii. After taking my oath of office at a PHS office in San Francisco, a few days later I had an appointment with my academic advisor, Professor Vincent Rogeveen (my first hearing of this unusual name). When I mentioned my future plans, he got quite animated—he was a PHS engineer during World War II! Naturally, I then asked him where he served and what he did. He said it was in New Orleans and his job was to track down the prostitutes around the waterfront district to come in and get "their shots." What?!

I knew my recruiter was the engineering director of the Portland area of the Indian Health Service, and I was sure my work wasn't going to be anything like that. But it did alert me to that standard service clause "…and other duties as assigned."

Bremerton's War Years

West of Seattle across Puget Sound, is Bremerton, founded in 1891 by William Bremer, who convinced the US Navy to purchase some of his waterfront on Sinclair Inlet, for building a Navy base. This eventual base was later joined next door by a naval shipyard. (I lived in the area for twenty-four years, first at a lake just out of town, and then in Bremerton proper, before moving to Gig Harbor, thirty miles south. Gig Harbor is on the west end of the earlier, infamous "Galloping Gertie" bridge that connected with Tacoma and that collapsed in a windstorm in 1940.)

A local historian, Suzanne Arness, once told me that Bremerton was fairly unique. While its population for a long time now has been around 40,000, earlier during World War II it was at least 80,000, maybe even closer to 100,000, due to its 24-hour, three shifts a day work at the shipyard and base. Workers lived in every spare bedroom, large closet, and habitable chicken coop that the US Navy could track down. The city next to the base and shipyard was a lively place with bars, brothels (twelve, at least known), USO dance halls, etc. Since the war, many of its residents are now retired and some are active-duty Navy personnel and similar shipyard workers. For many years at least one aircraft carrier has been home-ported there along with a complement of supply ships. At a Navy exposition in Bremerton, I once saw an article that Johnny Carson served there during the war as an Ensign aboard the battleship USS PENNSYLVANNIA.

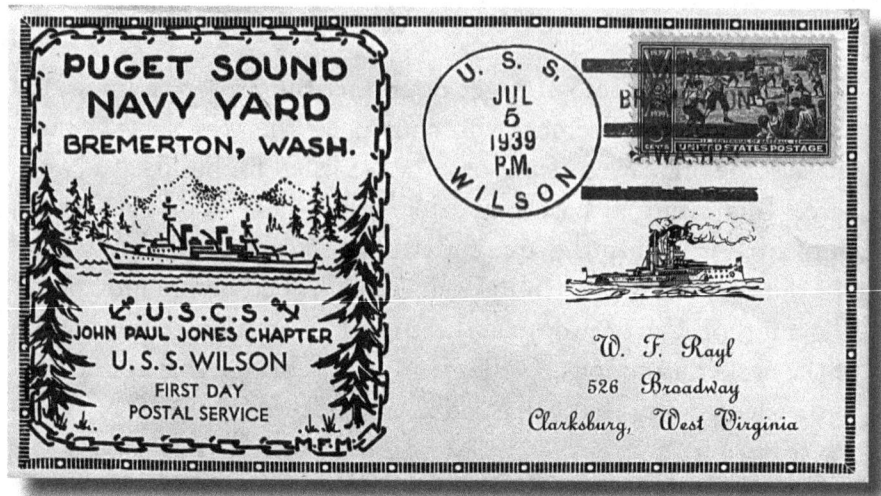

Figure 33: Early letter with cachet from Puget Sound Navy Yard in Bremerton, Washington (Author's Collection)

A local legend is that at the end of World War II, President Harry Truman was the guest of honor in a parade down Main Street in downtown Bremerton, and out of a second story window of the Eagles Club, some fellow shouted the now famous "Give 'Em Hell Harry!" After the war, the famous USS MISSOURI battleship, where the formal Japanese surrender on September 2, 1945, was conducted, was tied up at the Bremerton Navy Base for many years, and I was fortunate to have toured it twice before it was repositioned to Pearl Harbor in the 1990s. It is now docked close to the USS ARIZONA Memorial in Pearl Harbor, a fitting set of bookends to World War II.

Remembrances from Vets

At my mother-in-law's retirement residence in Gig Harbor, Washington, I met several older World War II veterans with riveting stories of the war. One, RC Buckland, was a Navy medical corpsman and for a while was stationed in Bremerton's Puget Sound Naval Shipyard. Early in the war, he and the other medics were in full charge of the base dispensary's day-to-day operations, even writing prescriptions. Life was good until the Navy nurses showed up, likely due to the arrival of seriously wounded servicemen, and everything changed.

The nurses ran a tight ship, even having the medics mop the floors, all to their dismay. Later in the war, while still in Bremerton, RC was assigned to the psychiatric ward of the hospital. He said working there during the daytime was alright, but the nights were horrible with so many military patients afflicted with what we now call Post-Traumatic Stress Syndrome. Nights there with frequently screaming patients were hellish for everyone.

RC humorously reminisced about once walking back to base after a night on the town and being met at the gate by a military policeman, likely a Marine. After his identity was checked, RC thought he was good to go, but the MP was suspicious and took a hard swing with his night stick at RC's belt buckle—and busted the bottle of booze that he thought was carefully hidden inside his pants. That likely smarted in more ways than one.

Once, I had the opportunity to meet a retired US Marine officer (name forgotten), living with his wife on the Olympic Peninsula of Washington. He had an absorbing story about his father in World War II, in charge of officer recruiting for his branch of service on the West Coast. His father got regular phone calls from Mrs. Eleanor Roosevelt, asking him to recruit specific men by name as officers. As this was the US President's wife, he expeditiously ordered standard background checks on each of these men prior to contacting them. In each case, the background checks revealed every one of these men to have a certain behavioral preference and, therefore, according to the military, "unfit for service." To me this was a unique, privileged insight to the personal interests of a famous person associated with our government, especially relating to wartime matters.

On the east side of Hood Canal (a fjord carved by ancient glaciers, now separating the Olympic Peninsula from the Kitsap Peninsula), I once went to a Sunday brunch with a friend at a well-known bed and breakfast venue. This house, with a long dock into the Canal (actually a misnomer, originally named a "channel" by one of Puget Sound's early explorers), overlooked the snow-capped Olympic Mountains to the west. It was called the "Wilcox House" in honor of a previous owner, Marine Colonel Julian Wilcox, who was the military's liaison with Hollywood during World War II when movies were scripted and filmed about the war.

After our meal, we were free to explore a bit in this large, modest art-deco, brick house. We soon located some unique rooms—suites named for Wilcox's occasional Hollywood visitors: Errol Flynn, Clark Gable, Spencer Tracy, and Ernest Hemingway! Another was an intimate, all-wooden bar with four stools and an adjacent pool room.

Back in the bar, we sat on the bar stools for a bit feeling pretty special, imagining we were sharing drinks and wild tales with the ghosts of these larger than life, famous characters. (After the death of his third wife, Carole Lombard, Clark Gable joined the Army Air Corps as a tail-gunner in World War II and ended the war as an Army Major.)

Back in Bremerton, again enjoying my weekly ping-pong games, I had a talk with another of our regulars, Craig Mecklenburg, an older gentleman who could still play a devastating game. He remembers as a young boy living in Bremerton, riding the ferry to and from Seattle during the war, the boat always slowing down considerably, as the submarine nets in Rich Passage, leading into Sinclair Inlet, had to be pulled back to allow for the ferry's passage. These nets protected the vital World War II activities at the base and its shipyard from enemy submarines. Fortunately, no enemy submarines were ever known to have entered Puget Sound, although on Hood Canal to the northwest of Bremerton there now exists a huge US submarine base, locally referred to as "Bangor," that homeports half of the US' strategic, nuclear-armed Trident submarine fleet.

On Bainbridge Island, just north of Rich Passage and the submarine nets, is another World War II installation of note. This was Fort Ward, started in 1938 to house a high security, top secret Navy unit that intercepted and decrypted high level Japanese naval transmissions. Before that, the base was an Army coastal artillery battery from 1890 that first protected the Bremerton naval facilities during World War I. In 1959, it was turned back to the army to monitor Korean and Soviet radio transmissions. What remains of the facilities today is now an obscure, overgrown city park with many happy deer, squirrel, and racoon residents.

The War Hits the West Coast

Turning south, there are the accounts of Japanese attacks along the Oregon and California coasts. The first was on February 23, 1942, when a Japanese submarine surfaced one night off the coast of Santa Barbara, California and from its deck gun, fired about a dozen shells at an inland oil field and refinery, thankfully hitting nothing of importance and causing no casualties. Two days later, local hysteria precipitated the "Battle of Los Angeles" when the release of large, silver-colored US weather balloons was mistaken for a follow-up attack by Japanese planes, resulting in live firing by US gun emplacements along the coast. Unfortunately, five Americans died in the ensuing excitement and chaos that followed—all apparently from heart attacks. The movie *1941*, staring John Belushi and Dan Akroyd, is a spoof of this event.

A second incident, believed to be in retaliation of the earlier, symbolically successful Doolittle Raid on Tokyo in April, was on June 21, 1942, when another Japanese submarine surfaced one night off the Oregon coast, just south of the Columbia River's mouth, and fired, this time on the US Army's shore batteries at Fort Stevens.

Again, nothing was damaged, but the soldiers there were outraged—however, not as you would think. The Army's commanding officer there forbade any return fire at the submarine for fear of giving away the fixed location of the US guns, but he was later commended for his good judgement by his superiors. (Most likely no cannon fire at a hostile target was ever fired from this fort, before or after this incident. I've toured the remains of this out-of-the-way, World War II site, seemingly enjoyed by more quadrupeds than bipeds.)

In September 1942, a plane catapulted from an off-shore Japanese sub, carried out two flights over southern Oregon, releasing incendiary bombs over forests north of Brookings on the coast, with little damage—no doubt largely due to Oregon and Washington's notoriously wet, coastal climate.

Japan also utilized a unique bombing strategy much later in the war. Using the high-altitude Jet Stream comprised of fast moving, easterly winds over the Pacific Ocean, Japan launched an estimated 9,000 incendiary balloon bombs (called *Fu Go*, or "fire balloon" in Japanese) headed to the US mainland. Many came down in the Pacific, but about 340 of them made their way over Canada and the US, causing fires and some electrical grid knockouts. The furthest east landed near Detroit, Michigan, but it's thought many others came down in remote, unpopulated locations and were never reported. From this unusual onslaught, Oregon had its third but final taste of Japanese warfare on its home front.

On May 5, 1945, outside of Bly, Oregon (about 50 miles east of Klamath Falls), a church picnic ended tragically when a downed balloon bomb in a tree was disturbed and exploded, killing Rev. Archie Mitchell's pregnant wife, Elsie, and five Sunday school children. News of all the balloon attacks was officially censored by the United States until after the war in order to not alert Japan to the limited success of the balloon bombs—a preventable tragedy for this family, but strategically understandable. Elsie Mitchell is buried in the Ocean View Cemetery in Port Angeles, Washington, and it's reported that Japanese occasionally visit her grave out of respect.

Later, Japanese military strategists proposed arming the balloons with anthrax and Yersinia pestis (plague) for biological warfare, but fortunately it was never implemented, although interestingly, plague is naturally endemic to the "Four Corners" area of the southwest US. Actually, in Europe the Allies used similar balloon bombs over Nazi Germany between 1942-44, although with unknown success...possibly the origin of the later Japanese *Fu Go* onslaught?

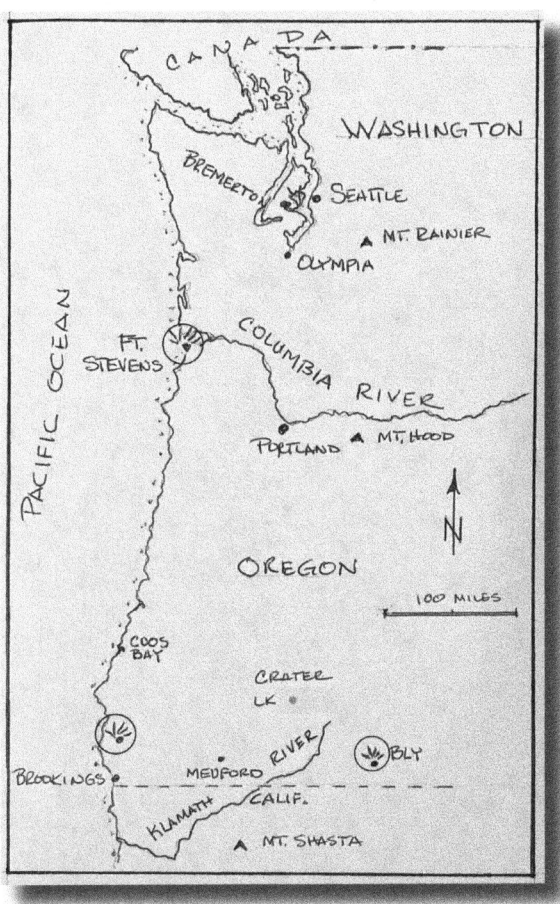

Figure 34: Sites of Japanese Bombings in the Pacific Northwest

CHAPTER 8

The War's Toll on the Japanese

My accounts about Japan in the war are, not surprisingly, somewhat limited. Two come from interviewing older Japanese persons and fellow ping-pong players at the Bremerton Senior Center. Both Don Yamaguchi and Kimi Hamm were youngsters during the war, living in the big cities of Nagoya and Tokyo, respectively. They both remember the aerial bombings by American planes, and have vivid memories of fleeing for their lives with their families. The fires consumed large swaths of mostly wooden homes, packed tightly together in their cities.

Don Yamaguchi recalls his childhood experience in Nagoya, especially escaping from fires after the Doolittle Raid in April 1942, where his family hid in bunkers and where he was shielded by his mother. Other times later on, the family fled to bamboo forests in the area to escape and hide. On a happier note, he remembers during the American occupation he first tasted American cheese and liked it.

Stranded in Tokyo

Again an interesting story from my Hawaii friend, Kazuo Shirakawa, this time about his mother Sachie, the daughter of Mr. Okabayashi who was interned in Hawaii after the surprise Japanese attack (see Chapter 2). After she had graduated from McKinley High School in Honolulu before the war, she moved to Japan for further studies and was living in Tokyo working for a Japanese electronics company when the war started. Forced to remain in Tokyo, she endured years of chronic food shortages and survived the eventual US bombings of Tokyo, although a close friend of hers in Yokohama was badly burned in the bombings and resulting fires there. During her time in Japan, despite her US citizenship, she was fortunately fully accepted into Japanese society due to her Japanese ancestry, language skills, name, and family connections in Japan.

At some time, during or after the war, she married a Japanese citizen, Goro Shirakawa, who had been drafted in 1939 into the Imperial Japanese Army, but had been released early for a medical reason. Due to his earlier college education (in Japan) and a happy association with a local YMCA, and having numerous American friends before the war, he was glad to emigrate to Hawaii in 1953 with his American wife and two young children (Kazuo and his sister). He and his children became naturalized US citizens in 1961. He apparently never spoke of his wartime experiences in the Army, although Kazuo believes that although his ancestors were *samurai*, he was a peaceful man and probably didn't side with the war fanatics pushing the *bushido* warrior creed and may have been secretly opposed to the war.

Figure 35: 1946; Sachie, infant daughter Yoshiko, and Goro Shirakawa in postwar Japan (Shirakawa Family Photos)

Figure 36: 1953, Shirakawa Family arriving in Hawaii, now with son Kazuo, center front. (Shirakawa Family Photos)

Fire Tornadoes Over Tokyo

In the March 1945 firebombing of Tokyo, an estimated fifteen square miles of structures were caught up in flames and destroyed. In these, and the two atomic bombings, frequently huge fire tornados (aka "firenados, fire swirls, or fire devils"), were created that were intense and fast moving. (In the aftermath of the Great Kanto Earthquake, magnitude 7.9, of September 1, 1923, that ravaged Tokyo, Yokohama, and surrounding cities, many severe firestorms resulted due to the quake's mid-day timing, lunchtime cooking fires, and broken water mains. In one open Tokyo location where a huge crowd sought safety from the fires, a great fire tornado reportedly incinerated 38,000 Japanese inhabitants.)

America's Options

America had earlier plans for defeating Japan and ending the war. Although Japan's Navy and shipping were mostly destroyed or of limited use due to fuel shortages, Japan's ability in the main islands to still field more than 10,000 planes, many capable of *kamikaze* attacks; still numerous Imperial Army divisions available; and huge numbers of loyal militia possible from its millions of its population, had to be considered carefully if a US invasion (tentatively code-named "Downfall") were to happen.

The US's Pacific island assaults against the enemy, especially the most recent in Okinawa, and the Japanese resist-until-death tradition resulted in an estimated combined Allied and Japanese casualties from an invasion totaling several million. To America's military and political leaders, this was unacceptable.

The second option was a naval blockade of Japan and continued aerial bombing. But that could take years, and the long-term suffering of Japan's populace would also kill many millions from starvation and disease. That was also judged unacceptable.

Then, when the newly introduced option of atomic bombing, with its expected horrific results to force the surrender was considered, Truman agreed to it, with US Secretary of War, Henry Stimson, calling it the "least abhorrent choice." Both this decision's timing and Japan's surrender decision were due to Soviet Russia threatening to invade northern Japan soon with its customary brutality and long-term occupation. Russia had earlier destroyed Japanese forces in Manchuria and was now poised to invade Hokkaido, the northern-most of the Japanese main islands, despite US warnings to Stalin not to do so. When Soviet forces did take the northern Kuril and Sakhalin islands soon after, an estimated 376,000 Japanese were killed or went missing.

Convinced to Give Up

On a more positive note for Japan in the last days of the war and then in the postwar reconstruction of Okinawa, Thomas Taro Higa (last heard of in Chapter 6) had an important role. After returning from combat in Europe and having toured many of the US Japanese internment camps while helping recruit fellow *nisei* Japanese for the Army, Higa realized he could further uniquely help in the war effort, this time in the Pacific. When he heard about the planned invasion of Okinawa and the certain fight-to-the-death resistance of the Japanese Army and Okinawan residents, he knew his knowledge of Japanese and the distinctly different Okinawan language, due to his early years living in Okinawa and Japan, would be very important assets in saving lives.

Higa volunteered for the Okinawan campaign and was quickly transferred to the US Pacific forces readying for the Okinawa invasion and land battles to come. As the US forces eventually prevailed in the fierce fighting, remaining Japanese soldiers and Okinawan militia and civilians retreated to the many caves on the island, refusing to give up. It was here that Higa, still a US Army soldier but with Okinawan cultural and language ties, went unarmed into many caves, convincing many Okinawans to surrender to US troops, despite being indoctrinated before to be murderous "white devils."

After the war, Higa returned to Okinawa and was very involved in helping to rebuild Okinawa, in one instance having pigs from Hawaii sent to Okinawan farms. In 1983, the Okinawan government gratefully honored his work on behalf of the Okinawan people during and after the war. Back in America he performed similar work, helping to restore a number of Japanese communities in the United States damaged by the relocation experience and other challenges of the war. Higa was quite the caring humanitarian, as well as the patriot.

Surrender!

An account I read somewhere years ago, told of something very important happening during the last American air attacks over Tokyo. Soon after the devastating atomic bombings of Hiroshima and Nagasaki, Emperor Hirohito decided it was finally time to surrender despite the defacto ruling group of military leaders' strategic plan (*Ketsu Go*, "decisive" in Japanese,) to continue fighting, inflict great damage and increase numbers of US casualties.

They hoped this would eventually force the United States to negotiate a surrender much more acceptable to Japan, versus the unconditional surrender demanded by the US military. The Imperial Palace then was guarded against anyone leaving it without permission, to prevent communications contrary to the military dictatorship's wishes. But during one of the very last air raids on Tokyo, the city's and palace's electric power went out, and a trusted servant managed to escape with a recording of the Emperor's voice in his "Sacred Decision" to end Japan's resistance and accept defeat. When it was broadcast in Tokyo the next day, the Japanese people heard the voice of this "Living God" for the first time ever, and the military leaders were essentially forced to agree to the unconditional surrender. (The Japanese military had just decided to surrender, but in any event the emperor's historic, recorded speech was the final word.)

The surrender announcement was on August 15 and the formal surrender documents were signed on the USS MISSOURI battleship in Tokyo Bay. The only concession made to Japan in the surrender was having the Emperor remain as a figurehead. World War II was now finally over.

CHAPTER 9

American Medals of Honor

In 1943, at his earliest opportunity, Daniel K. Inouye, a Hawaii *nisei* Japanese, dropped his pre-medical studies and enlisted in the US Army, joining the all-Japanese 442nd Regimental Combat Team. His first combat service was in Italy, then France, where he earned a battle-field commission from platoon sergeant to second lieutenant. He was then transferred back to Italy where he bravely distinguished himself in combat while being seriously wounded, later having his right arm amputated. Despite many awards, he was not properly recognized for his overall gallantry during those years, but later was awarded the Medal of Honor (MoH) by President Clinton, along with nineteen other *nisei* servicemen from World War II.

When Hawaii was admitted as the fiftieth US state in 1959, Inouye soon became one of Hawaii's two new senators, ultimately serving for fifty years in Congress. In June 1966, I graduated from Roosevelt High School in Honolulu and Senator Inouye was our commencement guest speaker. Our luck in having him there was due to a unique connection—a senior class member's father, Rev. William A. Buford, was the Inouye family's church minister. Years later in college, I wrote Senator Inouye about the plight of our Native Americans and got a detailed, encouraging four-page response, in part leading me to my eventual career about five years later as a PHS officer, working twenty years with the Indian Health Service. My first wife, whom I married ten years after high school, was a daughter of Reverend William A. Buford and his wife, Elizabeth, a most gracious set of in-laws. Rev. Buford was also a World War II Navy veteran.

I once read a short story about Inouye's World War II fighting. In Italy, he was shot in the chest, but two silver dollars in his pocket saved him. Later when he was again wounded and had his right arm amputated, he got rid of those silver dollars. Interestingly, many years before I read that story, I had been carrying around two silver dollars too, and still do—one for my good luck and the other to give away to someone who needed more luck than I did or to celebrate something special.

Years later, my friend and former colleague, Harold Scott, told me of his much older brother, James Scott, born 1924, who was in the Army infantry fighting in Italy during World War II. Later, James was in mountain combat and got frostbite, but was able to recover in a hospital without losing his toes.

Many other American men fought in Italy but they were not necessarily in the same platoon with a young Texan and good marksman named Audie L. Murphy! Harold told me that his brother never forgot something remarkable about Murphy—he always seemed to be standing straight up when he was firing.

At the end of the war, Audie Murphy was 21 years old, had been wounded three times, and awarded many medals for bravery, including the MoH. He went on to make many full-length movies in Hollywood and was also a country music composer. But as with other war veterans, he was haunted and troubled until his death, having personally killed an estimated 200 enemy soldiers and witnessed the death of many fellow American fighters.

Around 2007, I became acquainted with a friend of the family of another MoH recipient also living in Bremerton, John D. Hawk, whom I was privileged to visit with fairly often. "Bud" as he wanted to be called, lived in western Washington state when he enlisted in the Army in 1943, two weeks after his high school graduation. Over in Europe, after his participation in the

D-Day landings of American, British, and Canadian forces, in "The Falaise Pocket," a huge victory for the US Army inland from the Normandy landings, Bud Hawk distinguished himself. With several voluntary solo forays under intense fire into an apple orchard, he observed a vital concealed enemy position, then returned each time to the US line to help direct fire. During this he was shot in the leg and still courageously ran back and forth between the orchard and US position. Soon after, he was personally instrumental in capturing more than 500 German troops in that battle. After recuperating from the leg wound, he returned to combat action and by war's end had been awarded four Purple Heart medals. After the war in Europe, he was informed of the MoH nomination. In July 1945, he was one of the few MoH recipients to have a US President (in this case Harry Truman) come to him for the presentation, which was held on the steps of the Washington state capitol in Olympia.

As I visited with Bud in his home, I heard him tell a few of his fascinating combat stories. Several times he was in very close combat with German tanks and infantry and once literally ran into a German Panzer tank with a real "thud." Through the top hatch, a German (likely the tank commander) appeared and looked down to see what the noise was, with Bud lying on the ground in front of the tank. I asked "And?" Bud replied, "I shot him and then got the heck out of there. German tank crews loved to run over live enemy troops and grind them into hamburger!"

Twice I drove Bud to the nearby Bangor Navy Submarine Base. Once was for a private reception with three Navy admirals, a Coast Guard admiral, and the base's Marine commandant. We parked in a space reserved for us, right in front of the commanding admiral's front door. Bud deserved every bit of respect he got, including being officially "piped on board" Navy ships equivalent to a Rear Admiral when a guest for occasional ceremonies. Another trip was to address a large group of graduating sailors, where afterwards he passed around his actual Medal of Honor, saying it belonged to all Americans.

He humbly described his World War II actions by simply saying, "I came when I was called and did the best I could." It was as modest and eloquent a response as could be imagined from this real gentleman.

In June 2007, my son and I were invited to a special award ceremony for Bud. In it, a representative of the French Consulate in San Francisco came to present Bud the French Legion of Honor medal, which Bud graciously accepted, and later joked in a private aside with a big smile, "It took them 65 years to find me?" Bud once gave me a ride in his old pickup truck, referred to as "El Dento" with its MoH license plates; I thought how honored I was and chuckled to myself, "Unless he hit a pedestrian in a crosswalk, I don't think the local police would pull over this hero for anything!"

*Figure 37: 2007, French Legion of Honor Ceremony.
Left to right: Joshua Keeler, Awardee John "Bud" Hawk, and Author
(Author's Photo)*

After the war, Bud attended the University of Washington and then worked as a schoolteacher and principal for many years in Bremerton. In 2009, he and eight other University of Washington alumni that were MoH recipients, including the famous "Black Sheep Squadron" leader, Gregory "Pappy" Boyington, were honored with a campus memorial. Bud was frequently the Grand

Marshal of Bremerton's annual Armed Services Day Parade, and when he passed away in 2013, a large crowd attended the memorial service, including Bremerton's mayor, our congressman, and the governor. Later. a local elementary school in Bremerton was renamed in his honor.

I always felt it was a privilege to have had any personal connection, however remote, to these men of most uncommon valor, character, and service to America.

Figure 38: Postwar First Day Cover with stamps honoring US Armed Forces (Author's Collection)

EPILOGUE

While interviewing the many contributors to this collection, reviewing my notes, writing, editing, and rewriting their accounts, it was natural to pause many times to reflect with considerable sadness. While World War I from 1914 to 1918 had been initially called "The Great War," World War II from 1939 to 1945 was, in reality, a much more devastating world war, with estimates of even more than 30 million dead, hopefully never to be repeated.

These wars' deaths, destructions, horror, genocides, atrocities, and starvation were so pervasive and immense that they touched every continent except Antarctica and South America. These wars even included coastal naval engagements like the "Battle of the River Plate" of 1939 in waters offshore Argentina and Uruguay and all oceans and major seas.

Yet, today, that war's memory is vanishing daily, as those who survived it are rapidly dying, along with their stories. We occasionally watch old movies, newsreels, and documentary video footage of battles, speeches, ruins, refugees, and concentration camps of 70+ years ago, but we really can't envision or imagine the reality of those distant, uncertain, and violent years. And then, ignoring history, we seem then to unknowingly approach, again and again, the dangerous conditions that produced these wars.

We must be reminded that there is still much evil in this world. The ego, greed, pride (personal, ethnic, or national), and megalomania of ancient tyrants and conquerors that remain in our DNA need to be curbed to preclude future wars, limited or extensive, made even more dangerous through the spread of modern weapon technology. To do this, we as responsible citizens (and hopefully voters) need to be ever vigilant of those vying to be our leaders, whether heads of state, lawmakers, influential advisers, or just populist figures.

We must keep aware of and weigh their beliefs and backgrounds and make sound judgments about whom we follow, where, and why. A prime example of this is Hitler's *"Mein Kampf."* Hitler wrote his manifest years before coming to power and told those who would 'listen' about his thoughts and plans of a society where the leadership is considered a living god or such, where blind and total obedience is expected.

Vital to becoming a vigilant citizen is an independent press, and other media that freely and unbiased cover and report facts that inform us. We also need a populace with a sound knowledge of history's disasters and successes and to understand why they occurred.

As writer and philosopher George Santayana wrote, "*Those, who do not learn history are doomed to repeat it.*" Let us hope the experiences and the stories of these two devastating world wars and other wars may help promote peace on this fragile Earth.

About the Author

Geoffrey S. Keeler

The author was born to civilian parents in Honolulu in 1948 later moving to California at age two and then back to Hawaii at age eleven, graduating from high school in Honolulu in 1966. He went on to receive a BS in physics from the University of Hawaii in 1970 and an MS in civil engineering from Stanford University in 1972, whereupon he became an active-duty, engineer officer in the Commissioned Corps of the US Public Health Service (PHS), one of the now eight uniformed services of the United States.

The first half of his PHS career was an assignment to the federal Indian Health Service with postings in Seattle, Washington; Redding, California; Window Rock, Arizona (capitol of the Navajo Nation); and a three-year, overseas detail to the Public Utility Agency of Guam.

Between his first two assignments, he was employed by the American Samoa Government's Department of Public Works, 1977–79, to implement an important well drilling program for the Territory. The second half of his PHS career was an assignment to EPA's Region 10 office in Seattle, WA, where he set up and managed construction grant programs for tribal water and wastewater facilities in Alaska, Idaho, Oregon, and Washington.

After more than thirty years of PHS active duty, he retired in 2006 as a Captain. (PHS is a "sea service", using Navy uniforms, customs, and ranks, but with different insignia.) He humorously notes that he worked and lived in all four hemispheres: north, west, south, and east; the last two courtesy of his Pacific island assignments. He is also grateful for the unique career opportunities for interesting work in various cultures and geographic settings and meaningful service to America's native populations. He now resides in Gig Harbor, Washington, where he enjoys travel, reading, his life-long interest in collecting historic postal material, and occasional trips back to his beloved Hawaiian islands.

BIBLIOGRAPHY

Boccaccio, Giovanni, *The Decameron*

Pacific Wrecks, https://www.pacificwrecks.com

Dixon, Boyd PhD, "Japanese Stragglers on Guam" Guampedia, https:www.guampedia.coom/japanese-stragglers-on-guam

Brokaw, Tom, 2004. *The Greatest Generation*. New York City: Random House

Crowley, Robert, editor. 2006. *What If? Eminent Historians Imagine What Might Have been*. New York City: G. P. Putnam's and Sons

Darnell, Laura Ziegler, Laura and Ted Ziegler's Biography (publication unknown)

Espenshade, Jr., Edward, editor, 1965, *Goode's World Atlas, 12th Edition*. Chicago: Rand McNally

Hoffman, Nicholas von, and Gary Trudeau, 1976, *Tales from the Margaret Mead Taproom*. New York City: Sheed & Ward

Kirchner, Paul, 2009. *More of the Deadliest Men Who Ever Lived*. Hypnagogic Press

Kitsap Sun, June 29th, 2007, "Merci Beaucoup, Bud"

Leth, Frances H., 1991. *Fifty Years Ago—December 7, 1941—The Day of Infamy* (publication unknown)

Navy Times, 2004. "Explosion of LST Started Second Pearl Harbor" May 17: p. 42.

Porter, Jeanne, 1979, *Time of Suspense* (publication unknown)

Raymond, Richard, 2001, *Glimpses of My Life*. Compiled by Sharon Bushell. (publication unknown)

Rush, Ralph. *Holocaust: Confirmation and Some Retribution* (publication unknown)

Tweed, George R. 2010, *Robinson Crusoe,USN: The Adventures of George R. Tweed RM1c on Japanese-held Guam*, Chicago: Westholme Publishing

INDEX

A

Adak Island, 41, 43, 45
Adams Jr., Marine Col. Henry Jackson., 39, 40
Adams, Christie, vii, 39
American Samoa, 56–58, 79, 103
American Samoa, 45
Anderson, Jim, 67
Apra Harbor, Guam, 18, 52
ARIZONA, USS, 10, 82
Arness, Suzanne, 81
ASTORIA, USS, 20, 35, 41
Australia, 32, 39

B

Bainbridge Island, Washington, 27, 85
Bangor Navy Submarine Base, 84, 97
banzai charge, 39
Bataan Death March, 38
Bellows Airfield, v, 11, 17
Bly, Oregon, 86
Boccaccio, Giovanni, vii
Boyington, Gregory "Pappy", 98
Bremerton, Washington, 45, 81, 82, 84, 96
Brokaw, Tom, ix
Brookings, Oregon, 86
Brown Tree Snake., 53
Buckland, RC, 82, 83
Buford, Rev. William A. and Elizabeth, 95, 96
Burton, Rev. Lawrence, 54
Bushido, 63

C

Calbom, John, 78
Cambridge American Cemetery, 75
Canton Island, 12, 13, 29, 57
Cape York, Australia, 33
Capone, Alphonse "Al", 46
Carson, Johnny, 81
Chamorro People, 50, 60
CHICAGO, USS, 34
China, 12
Chunn, Jack, 67, 68
Churchill, Winston, 4, 102
Clinton, President Bill, 95
Cobra, Typhoon, 43
Code Talkers, Native American, 46
Coral Sea, Battle of, 15, 20, 35
Corregidor, 38
Covid pandemic, vii, 57
Cruz, Anthony "Tony", 60–62
Cruz, Margery, 60

D

Damien, David, 50
Darnell, Laura, 62
Darwin, Australia, 32
D-Day, 67, 71
Diamond Head Crater, 13

Doolittle Raid, 85, 89
Duke of Windsor, also see Edward VIII, King, 3, 5
Dunkirk, Miracle of, 73

E

Earhart, Amelia, 6, 7
Edward VIII, King, also see Duke of Windsor, 3, 5
ENTERPRISE, USS, 20
Ewa Beach, 17
Executive Order 9066, 24

F

Falaise Pocket, Battle of, 97
Ferrero, Pamela, 70, 71
Fey, Judy, 75
Fire Tornados, Firenados, Fireswirls, Firedevils, 91
First Marine Raider Battalion, 40
Flynn, Errol, 84
Fort Stevens, Oregon, US Shore Battery, 85
Fort Ward, Washington, 85
442nd Army Regimental Combat Team, 22, 98
Foster's Beer, 33
France, 3, 66, 67, 98
French Legion of Honor, 98

"Frenchy," 72

G

Gable, Clark, 84
Garhart, Molly, 77
Gig Harbor, Washington, 104
Great Kanto Earthquake, Japan, 91
Green Bay Packers, 46
Guadalcanal, Soloman Islands, 39, 41
Guam Combat Patrol, 52
Guam Island, Mariana Islands, 29, 49-54, 60

H

Haack, Roland "Red", 30
Hadden, Les, 52
HALEAKALA, SS, 30
Hamm, Kimi, 89
Harmon MD., Robert, 33
Hart, Elmer, 42
Hawaii, Kingdom of, 14
Hawk, John D. "Bud," x, 96-98
Hemingway, Ernest, 84
Hickam Air Field, 11, 20
Higa Brothers, Alvin, Nolan, and Sam, 7
Higa, Thomas Taro, 7, 65, 92
Hilo, Hawaii, 80
Hirohito, Emperor, 40, 51, 96
Hiroshima, 48, 56
Hitler, Adolph, 1, 2, 3, 12, 46, 102
Hong Kong, 62
Honouliuli Internment Camp, 24
Hoover, J. Edgar, 40

Howland Island, 6

I

Incendiary balloon bombs, 86
Inklebarger, Stephen and Ida, 34
Inouye, Senator Daniel K., 95, 96
Issei, 25

J

Juhasz, Michele and Norbert, 73, 74

K

Kahanamoku, Duke, 13, 25
Kamikazi, 47, 91
Kanahele, 16
Kauai Island, Hawaii, 8, 16
Kawahara, Elvis, 22
Kawahara, Lloyd, 22
Keeler, Cecil H., 7-9
Keeler, Jack and Olga, 14, 18
Keeler, Joshua, v, 56, 98, 110,
Keeler, Mary S.. also see Stanley, Mary v, 8
Kennedy, Jr., Lt. Joseph P., 76
Kennedy, President John F., 76
Klous, Mathias Jr., 66, 67
Klous, Mathias Sr., 66, 67
Koops, Ben, 72, 73
Kunz, Sonia, 70
KUTTABUL, HMAS, 34
Kwajalein, 41, 54

L

La Grange, California, 8
52
LEXINGTON, USS, 20, 35, 36
Leyte Island, Battle of, 49
Liliuokalani, Queen, 14
Lombard, Carole, 84
Los Angeles, Battle of, 85
Lum, Maedene, 27
LURLINE, SS, 27
Lynne, Typhoon, 52

M

MacArthur, General Douglas, 38, 43
Maeda, Ralph, 25
Maeda, Raymond, 25
Makiki Heights, 23
Makin Island, 41
Malaysia, 34
MAMO, MV, 29
Manoa Valley, 14
Manzanar Internment Camp, 27
Maputo, Mozambique, Africa, 63
Mariana Islands, 6, 48-50, 55, 56
Martial law, 22
Martyn, David, vii
Marzan, Keith, 15, 74
MATSONIA, USS, 12
McCartney, Paul, 71
Mecklenburg, Craig, 84
Meisner, George, 78-80
Memorial Park of the Pacific, Honolulu, 20
Meredyth, Geoffrey, 34
Messerschmitt Me 262, Jet Plane, 68

Midget Submarine, Japanese, 17, 19
Midway Island, 29, 37
Midway, Battle of, 15, 20, 36
Mildenhall Air Force Base, 75
Miller, Major Glenn, 76
MISSOURI, USS, 48, 82, 94
Mitchell, Rev. Archie and Elsie, 86
Monte Cassino, 65
MONTERAY, MV, 29
Montgomery, Warren, 54
Moors, Harry, 59
Moran, Larry, 59, 60
Moran, Priscilla, 59, 60
Morrissey, Patrick, 56
Murphy, Audie L., 96
Mussolini, Benito, 1

N

Nagasaki, 48, 56
Navajo Code Talkers, 46
Nepoui Bay, 31
New Caledonia, 31
Niihau Island, Hawaii, 16
Nikumaroro Island, 6
1941, movie, 85
Nisei, 7, 92, 95
Nishikaichi, Shigenori, 16
Noonan, Fred, 6
Nouméa, 31

O

Ohrdruf Nord Concentration Camp, 74
Okabayashi, Sachi, 89
Okabayasi Store, Kaneohe, 24

Okinawa, 7, 42, 47, 92, 93
Olympia, Washington, 97
Olympic Club, San Francisco, 32
Olympic Peninsula, Washington, 83
Osaka, Japan, 7
"Otto," German panzer tank driver, 69

P

P51 Mustang Plane, 32
Pago Pago Harbor, 30, 57, 58
Papua-New Guinea, 33, 35
Pearl Harbor, 8, 11, 14, 20, 29, 33, 35, 82
Peleliu, 40
PENNSLYVANIA, USS, 81
Philippine Islands, 29,38,39,43, 44, 59
Poland, 12
"Popor," 34
Port Angeles, Washington, 73, 86
Port Moresby, Papua-New Guinea Island, 33
Porter, Jackson "Jack," 13, 26
Porter, Jacob, 12, 13, 29, 31, 31
Porter, Jeanne, 1, 12, 13, 26
Porter, Michael "Mike," vii, 26, 27, 33
Prüm, Germany, 75
Puget Sound, Washington, 69, 81, 82, 84

Puget Sound Naval Shipyard, 82
Punahou School, 15
Punchbowl Crater, Honolulu, 20
Purple Heart, 66, 97

Q

Queen's Hospital, Honolulu, 8

R

Raymond, Lawrence "Larry," vii, 20
Raymond, Richard "Dick" R., Navy Gunners Mate, 20, 35, 36, 41, 43, 48
Red Hill, Aiea, 17
Republic of the Marshall Islands, 49
River Plate, Battle of the, 101
Roggeveen, Jacob, 56
Roggeveen, Professor Vincent, 80
Roosevelt High School, 23, 78, 95
Roosevelt, Eleanor, 83
Roosevelt, President Franklin D., 48
Roozen, Lt. Colonel Tony, 44, 45
Ruger, US Army Fort, 11, 15
Rush, Ralph, 74
Russia, 92
Russo-Japanese War, 1

S

Sacred Decision, Japanese, 94
Saipan, Mariana Islands, 50, 55
Samoa Islands, 56
San Francisco, 8, 32, 48, 70, 80, 98
Santa Barbara, California, 85
SARATOGA, USS, 17
Savo Island, Battle of, 41
Sax, Norma, vii
Scott, Harold, 96
Scott, James, 96
Seabees, US Navy, 47
Seattle, Washington, 2, 27, 44, 54, 81, 84, 103, 104
SERPENS, USS, 41
Shafter, US Army Fort, 11, 18
Shimasaki Family, 57
Shirakawa, Goro, 90
Shirakawa Family, 91
Shirakawa, Kazuo, 24, 89
Shirakawa, Sachie, 90
Shirakawa, Yoshiko, 90
Sidney Harbor, Australia, 34
Sierra Nevada Mountains, 8, 27
Simpson, Wallis Warfield, 3
Singapore, 34
South China Sea, 42
Spain, 4
Spanish Flu pandemic, v, 57
Stalin, Joseph, 1, 92
Stanford University, 1, 40, 80, 102
Stanley, Miriam Frances Louise Bawden, 4, 5
State, Muriel, 77, 78
Stevenson, Robert Louis, 59, 60
Strom, Peter, 39, 45, 46

T

Tarawa, 41
Tinian Island, Mariana Islands, 48, 56
Tokyo, Japan, 85, 89, 94
Totenkopf Insignia, 72
Tracy, Spencer, 84
Truman, Vice-President and President Harry, 48, 82, 84, 92, 97
Tsunami, 80
Tule Lake Internment Camp, 27
Tutuila Island, American Samoa, 30, 56
Tutuila Naval Station, USS, 57
TUTUILA, USS, 41
Tweed, George R., 49

U

University of Hawaii, 80, 102
University of Washington, 98
US Cadet Nurse Corps, 77
US Public Health Service, (USPHS), 61, 77, 80, 102

V

Vailima, Samoa, 60
Vietnam, 42
Viper, Typhoon, 44

W

Wake Island, 29
"Walter," 2, 3, 70
Ward, Navy Fort, Bainbridge Island, Washington, 90
Weiss, Julie, 30
West Loch, Pearl Harbor, 23
Wheeler, Army Air Field, 11
Wilcox, Colonel Julian, 84
World War I, 11, 23, 26, 85, 101
Wright, Edward, 41, 43

Y

Yacko, John, 42
Yamaguchi, Don, 89
Yokoi, Sgt. Shoichi, 52
YORKTOWN, USS, 37

Z

Zafft, Victoria, 70
Ziegler, Ted, 62, 63

www.ingramcontent.com/pod-product-compliance
Lightning Source LLC
Chambersburg PA
CBHW050327120526
44592CB00014B/2079